A
GOURMET'S
GUIDE TO

COFFEE

&

TEA

A GOURMET'S GUIDE TO

COFFEE
&
TEA

LESLEY MACKLEY

Photography by
SUE ATKINSON

HPBooks
a division of
PRICE STERN SLOAN
Los Angeles

ANOTHER BEST SELLING VOLUME FROM HPBOOKS

HPBooks
A division of Price Stern Sloan, Inc.
360 North La Cienega Boulevard
Los Angeles, California 90048

9 8 7 6 5 4 3 2 1

By arrangement with Salamander Books Ltd., and Merehurst Press,
London.

This book was commissioned and directed by Merehurst Limited.
Ferry House, 51/57 Lacy Road, London SW15 1PR
Photography: Sue Atkinson
Home Economist: Carole Handslip
Stylists: Maria Kelly & Carolyn Russel
Color separation by Kentscan, England
Printed in Belgium by Proost International Book Production, Turnhout

Library of Congress Cataloging-in-Publication Data

Macklely, Lesley.
    A gourmet's guide to coffee & tea / by Lesley Mackley
        p.   cm.
    Includes index.
    ISBN 0-89586-804-0
    1. Coffee.   2. Tea.   3. Desserts
II. Title.   III. Title: Gourmet's guide to coffee & tea.
TX415.M32   1989
641.6'373—dc20   89-15278
                                                          CIP

Contents

NOTES FOR RECIPE USERS

All spoon measures are level.

Whenever possible unless otherwise suggested, use fresh coffee
made with ground coffee for optimum flavor.

With regard to strength of coffee used in recipes:

Normal strength coffee = 1 tablespoon ground coffee or
1 teaspoon instant coffee granules to 3/4 cup water.

Strong coffee = 1 tablespoon plus 1-1/2 teaspoons
ground coffee or 1-1/2 to 2 teaspoons instant coffee
granules to 3/4 cup water.

Double strength coffee = 2 tablespoons ground coffee or
2-1/2 teaspoons instant coffee granules to 3/4 cup water.

Introduction

Wars have been fought and fortunes have been won and lost over tea. Songs have been written about it and holidays have been ruined by the lack of it. Its uplifting, soothing qualities and refreshing taste make it the perfect drink for any time of day and any occasion.

Coffee, like tea, is enjoyed all over the world for its reviving properties and its importance as the center of many social activities.

Coffee is also a valuable ingredient in cooking, its sophisticated flavor lending itself to a wide variety of delicious recipes. In this book you will find dishes showing the many ways in which coffee can be used. There are also recipes using tea as an ingredient, including such classics as tea sorbet, and new and unusual ways of serving tea and coffee drinks.

History of Tea

There are as many legends surrounding the origins of tea drinking as there are for coffee. The most popular tells of the Chinese Emperor, Shen Nung, in 2737 BC. He was boiling his drinking water under a tree, *Camellia sinensis*, when some leaves fell into the pot. The emperor was so delighted with the brew that he began to cultivate the plant.

Although it is thought the plant originated in India, the earliest recorded evidence of its cultivation comes from China in the 4th century. At that time, however, the leaves were not brewed as a drink but made into cakes and boiled with rice, spices or nuts. Later the dried leaves were powdered and whipped into hot water, rather like cocoa. The infusion of tea leaves in boiling water, which we know today, did not become fashionable until the Ming Dynasty, from 1368 to 1644.

Tea drinking spread from China to Japan where an elaborate tea ceremony evolved, but it was not until 1620 that tea was seen in Europe. The Dutch brought it to Holland from their trading stations in Java and Sumatra, and from Holland small amounts were sent to France and Britain. The Dutch and English soon established a regular sea trade, and the Russians sent overland camel caravans.

In 1669 the East India Company, granted a charter by Elizabeth I, brought China tea back in their cargo for the first time. Nine years later they began importing tea in earnest and held a monopoly until 1833. The Tea Act of 1773 enabled the East India Company to trade directly from China to America, cutting out the European exporters and American importers. This change in the law and the tax on the colonies resulted in the Boston Tea Party of 1773, when the citizens of Boston boarded the East India Company's ships and emptied their cargoes into the sea. Eventually war was declared.

When tea was first introduced into Britain in 1645, it was known as cha from the Cantonese word for tea *ch'a*. Even today in England it is not unusual to hear their national drink referred to as a cup of cha. By the end of the 17th century, the drink was known as tay or tea from the Amoy word for tea.

When tea first appeared in Europe, it commanded extremely high prices and was a novelty drunk only by the very wealthy. Heavy taxes increased the prices even further and inevitably smuggling became a thriving industry. Taxes were reduced in 1784 and tea soon became a popular drink with everyone. During the 18th century it even began to replace ale at the English breakfast table.

Coffee houses, which were flourishing in London at the beginning of the 18th century, were quick to spot the potential of the new beverage and there were soon over 500 coffee houses selling tea. This caused great dismay among the tavern keepers as they watched their customers desert them for the coffee houses. It also gave the Government cause for concern as the revenue from taxes on wine and liquor decreased. King Charles II declared coffee houses to be center of sedition and intrigue and made it illegal to keep a coffee house but, as this caused such bad feelings among his subjects, the law was never really enforced.

King George II enjoyed tea immensely and during the second half of the 18th century tea gardens, such as Vauxhall and Ranelagh, opened in London as places where fashionable society could drink tea, be entertained and, above all, be seen.

Cultivation of tea in India began in the 1820s when it was found growing wild in Assam by Major Robert Bruce. Tea plantations quickly spread throughout India and Ceylon and the first tea from India arrived in England in 1838. Its popularity quickly overtook that of China tea.

In Queen Victoria's reign, the first China tea of the season, which landed in London, commanded particularly high prices. This caused great rivalry among the shippers and a desperate search for the fastest sailing ships. The Americans designed the first three-masted fully rigged clippers to operate commercially and the first one cut the return journey time by

Silver tea pot with stand and burner

Traditional carved wooden tea caddy and spoon

German decorated china tea service

Antique silver tea strainer

half on its maiden voyage. The first British clipper was launched in 1850 and the Clipper Races from China to the Thames captured the public imagination and became an important sporting event.

Afternoon tea was an important social occasion in Victorian and Edwardian times. Tea drinking has continued as a social activity and nowadays is as popular as ever.

Young tea plant—Camellia sinensis

Growing Tea

Tea comes from the *Camellia sinensis* plant, which is a member of the camellia family. It is an evergreen with stiff, green, shiny, pointed leaves and delicate, fragrant white flowers. Left to itself the plant, which is strictly speaking a tree, would grow to a height of 50 feet or more, but it is pruned to a height of about 5 feet and the top is trained and pruned into a flat picking table.

New bushes are grown mainly from cuttings which are nurtured in shaded nurseries until they are 3 years old and ready to plant. The young plant is ready for harvesting at between 3 and 5 years old, depending on the plantation's altitude.

The tea plant is grown commercially only in the tropical and subtropical areas of the world. It needs a warm wet climate with at least 50 inches of rain a year and grows at altitudes of between just above sea level to 7,000 feet. As with coffee, the finer quality tea is grown at the highest altitudes where growth is slower and a small crop is produced.

The best tea is made from small young shoots and unopened leaf buds, with the choice pick being the terminal bud and the two adjacent leaves. In cooler climates the bushes are picked five times in 7 months, but in the tropics picking can take place every 7 to 10 days during the harvesting period.

Picking, which is mainly done by women, is extremely labor intensive. No machine can match the skill of an experienced picker who can gather 60 to 77 lbs. of leaf in a day. This is sufficient to make 16-1/2 to 20 pounds of manufactured tea.

Tea Growing Areas

Tea is grown all around the world in regions with a warm tropical climate and good rainfall. The main tea growing countries are as follows:

China: Although China is a major tea producing country, it is now mainly known for specialty blends.

India: 30% of the world's tea is produced here, in three main areas:

Assam: In this area, which covers the whole of the Brahmaputra valley, there are 650 tea estates. Tea is harvested from March to October.

Darjeeling: There are more than 100 estates in the foothills of the Himalayas producing what is known as the champagne of teas. The tea grown here is picked between April and October.

Niligri: This area, on a hilly plateau in southern India, is second only to Assam as the major producer of Indian black teas.

Sri Lanka: Tea estates replaced coffee estates in Sri Lanka, or Ceylon as it was called. Tea grown in Sri Lanka falls into 3 categories:

Low grown: from estates in the tropical rain forest of the island.

Middle grown: known as mid-country tea with good color and strength.

High grown: famous for lightness and flavor.

Indonesia: The Dutch began the tea trade in these islands. Trade declined after the Second World War, but once again this is now an important area, producing light fragrant teas mainly used for blending.

Kenya: The fertile land and favorable climate enable picking to take place all year. One-third of all tea imported into the UK comes from Kenya.

Malawi: This country was the pioneer of the tea trade in Africa and produces tea highly acclaimed for its color and brightness.

Tanzania: As in Sri Lanka, tea is grown at varying altitudes, producing teas with distinctly different characteristics which are mainly used for blending.

Zimbabwe: Although Zimbabwe only has an annual rainfall of 26 inches, irrigation enables tea to be grown.

Tea is also grown in a number of other countries, including Argentina, Brazil, Turkey, Iran, USSR, Malaysia, Japan, Taiwan, Vietnam, Popul New Guinea, Rwanda, Uganda and Zaire.

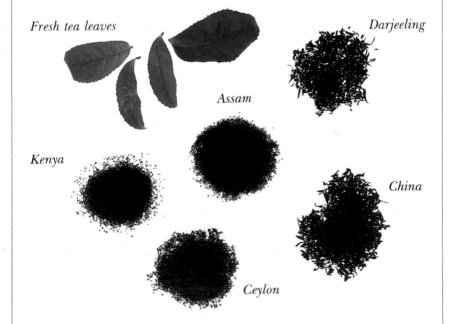

Fresh tea leaves

Darjeeling

Assam

Kenya

China

Ceylon

Processing Tea

The freshly plucked leaves are swiftly transported to the factory on the estate where they are processed into black, green or oolong tea.

Black Tea

There are four stages in the production process.

Withering: The shoots are spread on racks to dry to the point where they become withered and limp, having lost 50% of their moisture. This takes a day in the open air, but just a few hours in a drum drier.

Rolling: Rolling used to be done by hand and was the most laborious part of the whole process, but nowadays the withered leaves are machine rolled for an hour or two to break up the cellular structure, causing the chemical components of the leaf to be mixed together. During this process, the color, flavor and astringency of the finished tea begins to develop. Rolling also gives the leaves a twist which delays the rate at which they release their essence in the hot water during tea-making.

Fermentation: Oxydization is a more accurate name for this process where the green sticky leaves are left for 1 to 3 hours in a cool, humid atmosphere to develop a coppery brown hue and characteristic flavor and astringency.

Drying: When fermentation has progressed as far as the tea producer desires, the leaves are dried in temperature-controlled chambers until they turn black and have a moisture content of about 5%.

Green Tea

In the processing of green tea, the leaves are scalded or steamed to prevent fermentation before rolling and drying. This preserves the color and yields a pale yellow brew with a mild, slightly bitter taste.

Oolong Tea

This is a compromise between black and green tea—it is fermented briefly, once before and once after rolling. The leaves are half brown and produce a tea with a slightly fruity aroma and flavor.

Sorting & Grading

Once dried, the leaves of black and oolong teas are sorted into grades by machines which vibrate them through different sizes of mesh. Grades are simply an indication of the size of leaf, not of quality. Consistency of size is important because small pieces brew much more quickly than large ones. There are three grades or sizes of leaf, and these in turn are divided into grades.

Leaf tea: This takes longest to release flavor. It is divided into three grades:

Orange Pekoe has long, thin, closely twisted leaves; orange refers to the color of the tips which are included in this grade.

Pekoe has more open leaves; Pekoe is Chinese for leaf.

Souchong has large, coarse leaves.

Broken tea: This releases its flavor more quickly than leaf tea and is ideal for quick brewing.

Broken Orange Pekoe and **Broken Pekoe** are the two grades available.

Smaller leaf tea: This brews quickly and is used in packet tea and tea bags. The three grades are:

Orange Fannings, Fannings and **Dust,** which is the finest size of tea particles, used in tea bags.

These grades apply to both China and India teas, but some Indian producers have started to cut the leaves by machine. These leaves are known as legge cut. They are quick to infuse and are particularly suitable for the tea bag industry.

Strictly speaking, all black and oolong teas are broken to a certain extent during rolling or cutting in order to break their veins and release the natural juices of the leaf.

Green teas are graded according to age of leaves and preparation:

Gunpowder tea. Small tight balls of young and medium age leaves.

Imperial tea. An older version of gunpowder tea, with larger, looser leaves.

Hyson tea. Long, twisted leaves of various ages.

Gunpowder tea

Imperial tea

China Black tea

China Oolong tea

Packing & Shipping

After sorting and grading the tea is packed. Although it is sometimes shipped in paper sacks, it is usually packed into the traditional plywood tea chests, which are edged with metal for extra strength and lined with paper and foil to keep the tea fresh. Tea is either auctioned in its country of origin or shipped to the UK to the London auctions.

Blending

Having bought tea at the auction, the manufacturer then blends his own brand product for the retail market. A skilled tea taster tastes as many as a hundred samples of each consignment to ascertain which teas are required to make up a blend consistent with all those previously produced by the manufacturer. As many as 20 or 30 different teas will go into a popular blend and most contain three basic tea types: North Indian for strength, Ceylon for flavor and African for color and brightness, with others to complete the final taste.

Some specialist blenders will make up a recipe to your particular taste, or you could buy a selection of green and black teas and make up your own personal mix, as would have been done in the 18th century.

Types & Blends of Tea

Nowadays even supermarkets stock a wide range of specialty teas, each with its own distinctive flavor and aroma, whether it is a high quality blend or produced with leaves from a single area. Some teas are considered particularly suitable for drinking at certain times of the day. The following is a description of the main types of tea and blends.

Black Tea

Assam: The best grades have bright golden colored tips and are known as tippy Assam. The brittle black leaves produce a reddish tea with a brisk strong flavor which is ideal for breakfast and early morning. Serve with milk.

Ceylon: High grown Ceylon tea is considered one of the best teas in the world. Its golden color, full taste and delicate fragrance make it suitable for drinking at any time of day with milk or lemon. It is ideal for serving iced as it does not become cloudy when cold.

China Caravan: A blend of keemum teas, see below, with a distinctive, smooth taste. Serve mid-morning with a slice of lemon.

Darjeeling: A large leaf tea which requires 5 minutes to infuse. It has a rich flavor and bouquet reminiscent of muscat grapes. Darjeeling can be served at any time of day with milk or lemon.

Earl Grey: A blend of Darjeeling and China teas flavored with oil of bergamot. It is an ideal afternoon tea and should be served without milk or lemon as it has such a delicate flavor.

English Breakfast: This is usually a blend of Assam and Ceylon teas. With its strong full-bodied flavor, it is an ideal morning drink served with milk.

Irish Breakfast: Usually a blend of strong Assams, it is, as its name implies, an early morning drink.

Keemum: Fine quality China teas from Anwhei Province. With their rich, delicate flavor, they are less astringent than most teas and are most suitable for those with weak digestions. Drink with or without milk in the afternoon or evening.

Kenya: A fine flavor and astringency makes it very refreshing and uplifting at any time. Serve with milk.

Lapsang Souchong: The best quality comes from the Fukien Province in China. The distinctive tarry, smokey flavor makes it ideal for drinking without milk. A small amount blended with another tea will impart its pronounced flavor.

Rose Pouchong: This is from Guagdon on the southeast coast of China. Rose petals are mixed with the leaves to produce a very delicate, fragrant flavor. Serve in the afternoon without milk or lemon.

Russian: From the Republic of Georgia in Russia, which is why it is sometimes known as Georgian tea. It has a full-bodied flavor and should be served Russian style—strong with lemon.

Yunnan: From China's remote western Yunnan Province, this leaf produces a deep golden, clear, bright tea with a sweet delicate scent and flavor.

Oolong Tea

Formosa Oolong: One of the best and most expensive teas in the world. It has a large greenish-brown leaf, the best having silver colored tips. It produces a pale yellow liquid with a light peach flavor, which is best served without milk in the afternoon or evening or with an oriental meal.

Formosa Pouchong: The leaves are scented with gardenia, jasmine or yulan blossom and produce a pale delicate tea for drinking without milk in the afternoon or evening.

Green Tea

Gunpowder: The most popular of the green teas in the West. It has a fruity penetrating flavor and makes a pale straw-colored drink which goes well with Chinese food. It is also good served with mint.

Jasmine: A blend of black and green China tea perfumed with jasmine flowers. It is ideal for serving without milk or lemon to accompany Chinese food.

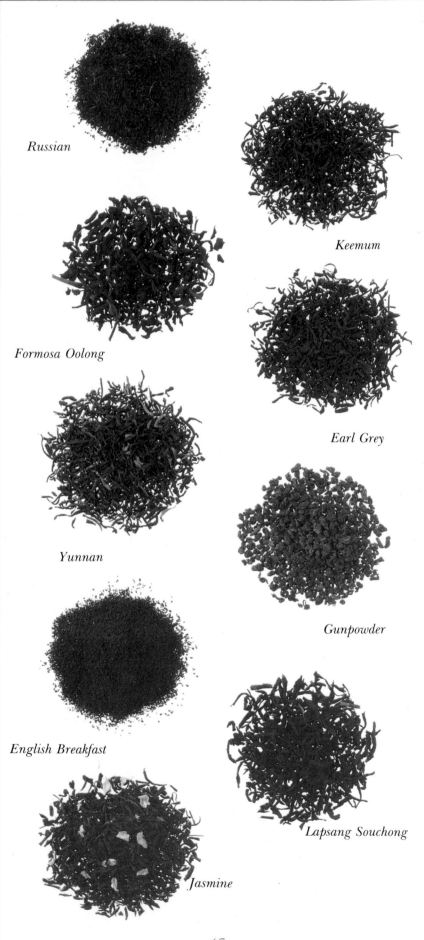

Russian

Keemum

Formosa Oolong

Earl Grey

Yunnan

Gunpowder

English Breakfast

Lapsang Souchong

Jasmine

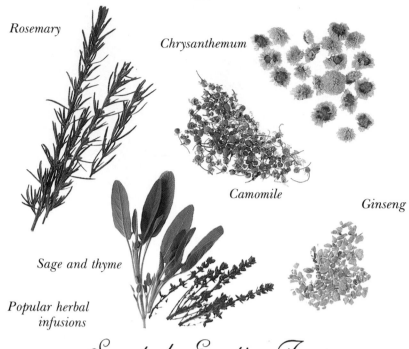

Rosemary

Chrysanthemum

Camomile

Ginseng

Sage and thyme

*Popular herbal
infusions*

Scented Exotic Teas

Scented and flavored teas are becoming increasingly popular and there is now a wide variety available in specialty shops. Best quality large leaf teas are flavored with natural oils, spices or dried flowers or fruit to produce teas which are light, refreshing and suitable for drinking at any time of the day, preferably without milk or sugar. Scented and flavored teas include:

Lemon—flavored with lemon peel.
Vanilla—sweet and fragrant.
Lotus flower—rich and exotic.

Mango—soft and fruity with a powerful flavor and bouquet.
Passion fruit—highly aromatic, flavored with passion fruit.
Tropical fruit—fragrant and exotic.
Spice—flavored with cinnamon and orange peel.
Japanese rice—subtle blend of Japanese green tea and rice.
Almond—blended with almonds.
Orange blossom—flavored with fragrant flowers.
Peach—with the scent and flavor of peach oil.

Infusions & Tisanes

Before the introduction of tea and coffee to Europe, herbal infusions—or tisanes as they are called on the continent—were popular. Today drinks made from herbs and plants are enjoying a revival. These infusions or tisanes are frequently called herb tea although they do not in fact contain any leaves from the *camellia sinensis* bush—unlike flavored teas which are made of tea blended with herbal leaves, such as sage or mint. They are, however, refreshing and soothing and are often thought to have beneficial medicinal properties.

Infusions are made in the same way as tea: boiling water is poured over the leaves and left to infuse for a few minutes. Milk is not usually added, although a little lemon juice or honey may help to bring out the flavor. Some of the more popular herbal infusions are:

Camomile—for easing aches and pains and inducing sleep.
Chrysanthemum—soothing and relaxing.
Elderflower—for soothing the nerves.
Rosemary and lemon balm—thought to stimulate the memory.
Sage and thyme—soothing for colds and sore throats.
Pennyroyal—for curing depression.
Ginseng—said to cure impotence.

Almond

Scented exotic teas

Vanilla

Lemon

Mango

Passion fruit

Japanese rice

Lotus flower

Spice

Tropical fruit

Peach

Making Tea

In order to enjoy tea at its best, it is worth taking the trouble to follow a few simple rules when making a pot of tea.

1. Use the best tea you can afford.

2. Fill the kettle from the cold water tap; hot or reheated water contains less dissolved air and has a flat, stale taste.

3. Warm the teapot by rinsing it out with hot water. This ensures that the water stays at boiling point when it touches the tea.

4. Add 1 teaspoon of tea or 1 tea bag per person and one for the pot. This means using 1 teaspoon of tea to every 6 fluid ounces of water.

5. When the water is boiling, take the teapot to the kettle and pour in the water. Replace the lid and let the tea infuse for 3 to 5 minutes, according to the size of the leaves; large leaves take longer to brew than small ones. Tea releases color before flavor and while the desirable color may be reached after barely 1 minute, it takes several more minutes to bring out the full quality of the tea. If this length of time results in too strong a flavor, then less tea should be used. Stir before pouring.

6. Serve the tea when it is freshly made as it will have a stewed taste if left in the pot for any longer than 10 minutes. Covering the pot with a tea cozy speeds up the brewing process, so is best avoided. Stewed tea can be avoided by removing the infused leaves from the water with a perforated tea ball or spoon or, better still, the tea can be decanted through a strainer into a second warmed teapot.

Tea Bags

In 1904 Thomas Sullivan, a New York merchant, invented a silk tea bag in which to send out samples. Nowadays the bag is made of odorless, tasteless filter paper. Half the tea used in American homes and three-quarters of that used in Britain is bagged. All major blends, some specialty teas and even flavored teas are available in bags; the tea they contain is of exactly the same quality as a packet tea of the same blend.

As much care is required when making tea with tea bags as with loose tea—simply dipping a tea bag in a mug of hot water will not produce a good cup of tea!

Serving Tea

Whether to serve tea with or without milk is a matter of continuing controversy. In America and on the Continent milk is not normally added, whereas in Britain it is quite common to add milk to most black teas.

As the milk is added, the tannins immediately bind to the milk proteins, making the taste less astringent. It would, however, be considered nothing short of sacrilege to add milk, or even lemon, to any green or oolong teas.

When to add the milk is also a matter for debate. If the milk is poured into the cup first it blends in more easily with the tea, but adding it afterwards does allow the individual to control the amount to his or her taste.

The habit of pouring the milk into the cup first dates back to the late 17th century when fine porcelain cups were introduced into Britain by the East India Company. Until then people had been used to drinking out of pewter or earthenware mugs and, unaware of the heat-proof properties of porcelain, were afraid that the china would crack if the hot tea was poured straight into the cup.

Delicately flavored teas served without milk are particularly refreshing on a hot day. The addition of lemon was a Russian habit, introduced by Queen Victoria's eldest daughter, the Princess Royal, who was the consort of the Emperor of Prussia.

Most teas can be served with milk or lemon; others are better without either. Tea bags are becoming increasingly popular; many teas are now available in this form.

Traditional English Royal Doulton tea service

Teapots & Cups

Teapots were brought from China into Europe by the Dutch and Portuguese in the early 17th century. Early British teapots were silver but by the time tea drinking became a national habit in the 19th century, a whole new business was created for the English pottery industry producing tea sets. Nowadays teapots are available in all shapes and sizes in a wide variety of different materials. A teapot made from almost any material will make good tea, but aluminum should be avoided as it makes the tea black.

When choosing a teapot, make sure that it is comfortable to lift without your knuckles touching the side of the pot. It should have a hole in the lid to allow air to enter the pot when tea is being poured, and there should be a protrusion on the lid to keep it in place while the pot is tilted.

It is a myth that a teapot lined with tannin makes good tea—in fact, it will make it bitter. To remove tannin, fill the teapot with hot water, add 4 teaspoons of bicarbonate of soda, stir to dissolve and let soak for several hours. Avoid using detergent or soap when washing a teapot as the lingering taste could spoil the tea.

The first teacups from China were tiny delicate bowls. Handles were added in the mid 18th-century and as tea became less expensive larger cups were made.

Chinese tea service

Japanese tea service

Chinese tea cups

Royal Derby china teapot

German teapot, 1860

French teapot, 1780

*Chinese porcelain teapot
(contemporary)*

Moroccan teapot (contemporary)

Chinese teapot, 1900

Traditional tea caddy and spoon

Tea-making Equipment

Tea Caddies

The word caddy originated from the Malay word *kati* meaning one pound—the amount contained in the small box in which tea was originally packed for export. In the 17th and 18th centuries caddies were always fitted with a lock and key to prevent their valuable contents being stolen. Some caddies contained several compartments for holding different teas and a mixing bowl in which to blend them.

As tea easily absorbs moisture and odors it is advisable to keep it in a caddy or airtight container where it will stay fresh for some time, although the flavor will begin to deteriorate after awhile.

Infusers

An infuser is a perforated metal container in which a measured amount of tea is placed. The infuser is placed in the teapot, the boiling water is poured on and it is left to stand for a few minutes. When the tea has infused the infuser is removed, preventing the tea from brewing.

Most infusers are made of stainless steel; aluminum should be avoided as it makes the tea black. The infuser must be large enough to allow the leaves to expand and give a good brew.

Teapot Cozies

Teapot cozies are padded covers for putting over a teapot to keep the tea warm. As they allow the tea to over brew and become stewed, teapot cozies should only be used when the tea is made with an infuser or tea bags, which can be removed when the desired strength is achieved.

Tea Strainers

The strainer spoon was once used to sift dust from the tea leaves before placing them in a pot. Nowadays a tea strainer is a perforated bowl which is placed over a cup to strain the leaves when the tea is poured through.

Lemon Squeezers

Lemon squeezers are designed to hold and squeeze a wedge of lemon into a teacup without any peel and seeds escaping.

Tea strainers

Lemon squeezers

Infusers

Customs & Ceremonies

Japanese Tea Ceremony

Of all the customs and rituals associated with the serving of tea, the Japanese tea ceremony *Chanoyu* is the most intriguing. Guests arrive at the tea house *(sukiya)* by a special path *(roji)* and prepare themselves for the ceremony in the waiting room *(yoritauk)*. They enter the tea room by crawling through a low doorway and are given a light meal *(kaiseki)* before returning to the garden or waiting room.

At the sound of a gong they return to the tea room where the tea master has everything ready for the ceremony. He cleans all the utensils then puts three scoops of green powered tea *(matcha)* into a bowl. He adds hot water from the kettle simmering by the fire and whisks it up to produce an emerald green frothy tea. The guest of honor sips the tea, wipes the rim of the bowl and passes it on to the next guest.

The tea master then makes a second infusion of thin tea which is served in individual bowls and leaves the guests to chat and gossip.

Moroccan Tea-making

Tea-making in Morocco is almost as much a ritual as in Japan or China. Mint tea is prepared with due ceremony in every home, café and place of work.

To make Moroccan mint tea, place 2 to 3 teaspoons of green tea into the pot, pour in boiling water, then quickly pour it out to remove dust. Pour in more boiling water and let stand 1 minute. Put mint leaves into the pot and let stand another minute. Add sugar, pour out one glass of tea, then pour it back into the pot.

After repeating this operation, the tea is served by pouring from a height into tiny glasses.

Utensils for Japanese tea ceremony: kettle, tea cup, bamboo whisk, matcha (tea) in bowl and napkin

Afternoon tea: scones and home-made jam accompany tea for this traditional English social occasion

Afternoon Tea

The Western custom of serving afternoon tea is of as much social importance as any other tea ceremony: It was introduced in the 19th century by Anna, 7th Duchess of Bedford. In those days lunch was early, but dinner was not served in the grand houses until 8:30 or 9 o'clock, so the Duchess of Bedford came up with the idea of serving tea with sandwiches and cakes in the middle of the afternoon. Taking afternoon tea soon became a very fashionable way for ladies to entertain and socialize.

Today, although our way of life does not allow us time to indulge in afternoon tea everyday, it is still a very pleasurable way to entertain and one in which all age groups can participate. As in the Duchess of Bedford's day, it is customary for the hostess to pour out the tea and pass it to the guests, who each have a cup and saucer and a small plate for sandwiches and cakes or scones.

Tea & Health

Tea contains half as much caffeine as coffee. Decaffeinated teas are available, but most people find that the amount of caffeine contained in tea gives a beneficial lift. Tea also contains theophylline and theobromine which act in a similar, but milder, way to caffeine and aid muscle relaxation.

Served on its own, or with lemon, tea contains no calories, but with milk added contains about 29 calories. Sugar adds 28 calories a spoonful.

History of Coffee

There are numerous legends surrounding the discovery of coffee. The best known is that of Kaldi, an Abyssinian goat-herder, who noticed one day that his goats were prancing about like young kids. He discovered that they had been nibbling red berries from a shrub growing on the hillside. He tried them himself and soon became as frisky as the goats! An abbot from a nearby monastery, observing this extraordinary phenomenon, gave some berries to his monks who were able to pray all night without falling asleep.

The more likely story of the discovery of coffee is that it was first noticed to have stimulating properties by wandering tribesmen in Ethiopia, where it certainly originated. At first the berries were eaten whole, or crushed to a pulp, mixed with animal fats and rolled into balls of food. Later the berries were made into a broth with water. After traders introduced coffee to the Arabs, the prophet Mohammed drank a kind of wine made from the fermenting pulp.

By the 13th century, the practice of roasting and grinding the beans to make an infusion had become popular in Arabia, and in spite of the Arabs' efforts to control the supply, pilgrims managed to smuggle out quantities of the green coffee beans. Coffee was soon being grown in all the areas surrounding Mecca and Medina, and by the 15th century its cultivation had spread to Persia, Egypt, Turkey and North Africa. Coffee houses sprang up everywhere and were soon criticized for being centers of immortality and vice, and accused of being responsible for turning people away from religion.

There were also problems when coffee was introduced into Europe following the arrival in Venice of the first consignment from Turkey. In Rome the clergy appealed to Pope Clement VIII to have coffee banned, calling it the Devil's drink, but the Pope liked it so much that he gave it his blessing. Soon the first European coffee houses opened and became popular meeting places for intellectuals and artists.

The first coffee house in England opened in Oxford in 1637. They quickly proliferated and began to play a part in political and literary life. Commercial life also flourished, with insurance companies such as Lloyds, newspapers, clearing houses and shipping exchanges owing their beginnings to coffee houses. Jonathan's in Change Alley was the birthplace of the Stock Exchange, and to this day attendants in the Stock Exchange are still called waiters.

Women were originally barred from coffee houses. In 1674, they published a petition in which they complained that coffee houses were tempting men away from home and that the drink made them impotent!

By the 18th century coffee was being grown by the Dutch in Java and the French were growing it in the Caribbean. The French were very possessive of the seeds, but a Brazilian spy seduced the wife of the Governor of French Guyana and she gave him sufficient coffee seeds to found Brazil's coffee industry.

Today, coffee is appreciated and enjoyed throughout the world, with each country having its own version of the original coffee houses. Coffee drinking is still an activity which tends to draw people together where they can chat and relax in a convivial atmosphere.

Growing & Producing Coffee

Coffee grows in a band between 25°N and 30°S of the equator where there is an abundant rainfall, an average temperature of between 65F to 75F (18C to 24C) and no frost.

Left to mature, the coffee plant would grow to a height of about 20 feet, but on coffee plantations it is pruned to a height of about 6 feet. The plant resembles a camellia bush and has dark, glossy, pointed leaves. The white jasmine-like flower is extremely delicate and highly scented. It takes from 3 to 5 years for the bush

to produce fruit. The fruit ripens several times a year and appears on the bush in various states of maturity; which makes mechanized harvesting virtually impossible. In Brazil, however, the climate enables all fruit to ripen simultaneously and harvesting is done by machine.

The fruit, or cherries, take 6 to 8 months to ripen from dark green to deep red. Each tree produces 2,000 cherries a year. Inside each cherry is a pair of coffee beans or occasionally a single bean known as a peaberry. The yield from 2,000 cherries is one pound of beans.

The beans are separated from the pulp and skin by one of two methods.

The wet method is used for hand-picked quality beans and is employed in countries with heavy rainfall. The cherries are pulped to remove the outer fleshy layer, then the beans are soaked and left to ferment for 1 to 2 days. They are then washed and dried, by machine or naturally in the sun. Finally, a hulling machine removes the thin parchment to reveal the green coffee bean.

The dry method is much simpler and is the oldest way of preparing coffee. The cherries are spread out in the sun for 2 to 3 weeks. They are raked and turned frequently so that they dry evenly. When completely dry, the cherries are hulled by machine to remove the skin and dried pulp.

Beans are sorted, picked over and graded by hand. Small samples are roasted and tasted by a coffee taster who determines the quality.

There are two major species of commercial coffee: *arabica* and *robusta*.

Arabica is the superior coffee, with a rich flavor and excellent aroma. Generally speaking, the higher the altitude at which coffee is grown the better the quality. Arabica is grown in high altitude areas where there is a good rainfall.

Robusta coffee plants flourish at lower altitudes and, as the name implies, are disease-resistant and quick-growing. Robustas are used for making instant coffee and are often blended with other beans.

The coffee is packed in sacks, then in special containers, designed to ensure that the coffee reaches its destination in perfect condition.

Coffee Growing Areas

Within the area in which coffee grows, there is a great variaton of climate, altitudes and soil conditions, all of which affect the flavor, quality and characteristics of the beans grown in each country.

Brazil produces 30% of the world's coffee. It is not the best quality and is mainly used to make instant coffee. Santos is the top grade with a mild, smooth flavor.

Cameroon produces mainly high quality robusta beans, with a small quantity of mellow arabica. Several other African states produce similar beans.

Columbia. All the coffee beans grown in Columbia are arabica. They have a rich, full flavor, ideal for all roasts. Medellin is one of the best-known coffees, with a well balanced acidity.

Costa Rica coffee is much prized for its fine rich flavor and sharp acidity. One of the most famous coffees is Tarrazu.

Dominican Republic coffee is known as Santo Domingo. The best grades are strong and full-bodied. They are popular in the United States and West Germany.

Ecuador coffee has a sharp flavor and thin body and is usually only used in blends.

El Salvador coffee is 100% arabica, but lacks the flavor and body usually associated with arabica. With its slight flavor and mild body, the coffee is similar to that of Guatemala, but of slightly inferior quality.

Ethiopian coffee is strongly flavored and often described as winey. It has a full body and excellent aroma. The best known is Harrar, which has replaced the Mocha from the Yemen. It is known as Ethiopian Mocha, or even just Mocha, although it lacks the really rich chocolately taste of the original Yemen bean.

Guatemala. The high grown coffees are mild with good acidity and aroma. The best are Coban and Antigua.

Haiti. The best grades have a rich, mildly sweet flavor. The inferior qualities are used for high roasts in Europe. Production is low due to general lack of enterprise.

Hawaii. The production of coffee is declining in favor of growing Macadamia nut trees. Nevertheless Hawaiian coffee, known as kona, is of superior quality: mellow, smooth and slightly acidic.

India. Mysore is the best known of the Indian coffees. It has a smooth, soft flavor and delicate aroma, and is often blended with Mocha. It is particularly popular in Scandinavia and France.

Jamaica. Blue Mountain is highly acclaimed as being the perfect coffee in terms of its smoothly balanced flavor, aroma, body and acidity. Most of it is sold in Japan. It is very expensive and rarely found outside specialist coffee shops.

Kenyan arabicas are of a very high quality with excellent full flavor and fine acidity, combined with mildness. The Kenya Peaberry is particularly prized.

Mexican coffee is light and rich with a fine acidity. The best variety is Coatapec. Most of the production goes to the United States.

Papua New Guinea. Coffee has only been grown here commercially since the 1950s, when it was sold mainly to the United States and Australia, but it is now becoming popular in Europe. The full smooth flavor resembles that of Kenya coffee.

Peru. Production is increasing, so this coffee is more widely available. It is mildly acid with a good flavor. The best known is Chanchamayo.

Sumatra and Java. These two countries produce sweet, mellow, full-bodied arabica coffee particularly popular with the Dutch. Robustas are now being produced in quantity but, although good, they are inferior to the arabicas, particularly those of Sumatra. The best grade is Mandheling, which is smooth and rich.

Tanzania. With its mellow flavor and slight acidity, this coffee is similar to that from Kenya, but it is less full-bodied. The best is known as Kilimanjaro, taking its name from the mountain on which it grows.

Venezuela. Meridas are the best of the Venezuelan Maracaibo coffees. They are of excellent quality—sweet, fine-flavored and light-bodied.

Caracas and Caracas Blue, with their distinctive flavor, are particularly popular in France and Spain.

Yemen. Mocha, named after the city of Moka, is the coffee produced in the Yemen. It has a distinctive, winey, piquant flavor and is very full-bodied. It is valued as an after-dinner coffee and is often blended with mild coffees, such as Mysore, Java and Sumatra. It is also popular for Turkish coffee blends.

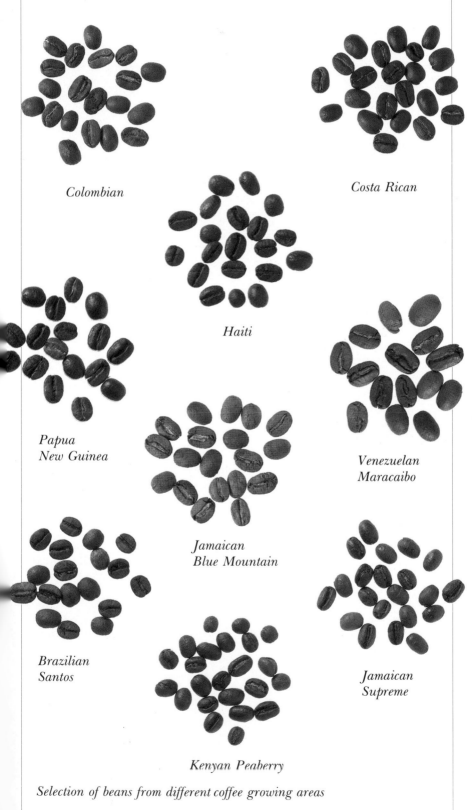

Colombian

Costa Rican

Haiti

*Papua
New Guinea*

*Venezuelan
Maracaibo*

*Jamaican
Blue Mountain*

*Brazilian
Santos*

*Jamaican
Supreme*

Kenyan Peaberry

Selection of beans from different coffee growing areas

The Different Roasts

Unroasted green coffee beans

The green coffee beans are roasted to develop their flavor and aroma. The degree of roasting determines factors such as the mellowness, richness and nuttiness of the brew; it does not affect the strength of the coffee. This is determined entirely by the proportion of coffee to water when brewing. During the roasting process, chemical changes take place; the beans release aromatic oils, caramel is formed and gases are released into the bean.

The higher the roast, the lower the acidity of the coffee. Therefore, for the dark roasts, cheaper growths are generally used. Choice growths would be wasted, as much of their aroma and original flavor would be lost. Degrees of roasting can be interpreted differently, but there are several which are recognized.

Light or **pale roast** gives a light-brown dry bean with a delicate flavor and aroma. It is used for mild beans whose flavor would be over-powered by a stronger roast. These coffees are particularly suitable for drinking at breakfast with milk added.

Medium roast gives a strong flavor, bringing out the characteristics of many coffees. It produces coffee which is perfect for drinking at any time of day, with or without milk.

Full roast produces dark-brown beans with a little oil on their surface. The coffee has a strong flavor with a touch of bitterness. It is suitable for drinking black or with a little cream, after lunch and in the afternoon.

High roast is also known as Double or Continental roast. The beans are shiny, oily and black. The coffee has a strong bitter kick and is served black after dinner.

Italian roast is also known as Espresso roast. This coffee is dark to the point of carbonization.

Light roast

Medium roast

Full roast after-dinner blend

High roast continental

Roasting at Home

Roasting coffee beans at home.

Some specialist coffee shops sell green beans, and with care it is possible to roast them at home. This is certainly the cheapest way to buy coffee and the best way of ensuring that your coffee is really freshly roasted.

There are electric roasting machines available for domestic use, but they are very expensive and would only be worthwhile if you regularly roast quantities of coffee.

Satisfactory results can be achieved by roasting the beans in a heavy-bottom skillet. The odors produced are quite strong, so it is advisable to have a window open or an extractor fan in operation. Cover the base of the skillet with one layer of green beans. Start off with a low heat, turning it higher towards the end. The quicker the roast, the better the coffee, but it is better to be a little cautious until you are experienced. Keep the beans moving constantly in order to brown evenly; they soon darken and occasionally pop open. Remove them from the heat just before they reach the desired degree of roasting, as the residual heat in the beans

causes them to go on darkening for a short time. Keep a small sample of commercially roasted beans to compare the colors the first few times you attempt your own roasting. When the beans are ready, tip them onto a cold surface to cool, and blow away the little pieces of chaff.

It is often suggested that roasting can be done in a hot oven, but as the beans really do need to be stirred constantly, it is not as practical as the skillet method. Oven roasting does, however, reduce the fumes in the kitchen.

Until you have become experienced, it is advisable to aim for a medium-brown roast as it is easy to burn the beans if they become much darker. Peaberry beans are the easiest to use as their round shape causes them to roll about easily in the skillet, becoming evenly brown.

One advantage of doing your own roasting is that you can experiment, adding spices such as cloves, cinnamon or cardamom to the coffee toward the end of the roasting.

Buying & Storing Coffee

Although good coffee is widely available in supermarkets, it is worth patronizing a specialist coffee shop. Not only will their advice and suggestions for different blends be invaluable, but you can be sure of buying coffee which is freshly roasted.

Green coffee beans keep indefinitely, although they may be affected by dampness and can absorb strong odors. Once roasted, however, the coffee beans immediately start to lose their aroma and will have lost it almost completely within 2 weeks. Some suppliers now pack coffee beans in bags which have a small valve to permit the escape of residual roasting gases while preventing air from passing back into the pack. This means that the coffee can be packed while fresh and warm from the roaster. It will stay fresh for up to 6 months.

Ground coffee loses flavor and aroma even more rapidly, and it is therefore important to buy coffee in small quantities when you need it and use it as quickly as possible, grinding it as required. Pulverized Turkish coffee deteriorates particularly quickly and should be used within 24 hours.

Coffee beans and ground coffee should be kept in the refrigerator in airtight containers. Coffee beans can be stored in the freezer for up to 1 year; they can be ground while frozen. Vacuum-packed ground coffee retains its freshness until the pack is opened. It should then be transferred to an airtight container and used within 2 weeks.

Grinding Coffee

Fine espresso grind

Fine grind

Medium grind

Medium coarse grind

Coarse grind

Before coffee can be brewed to drink it must be ground, and choosing the correct grind is essential. The fineness is dictated by the method of brewing to be used; the finer the grind, the greater the surface area of coffee exposed to the water and the longer it will take for the water to run through. The finer grinds are more economical.

A **coarse grind** is suitable for brewing coffee by the pot method.

A **medium grind** is the most versatile as it can be used for the pot method, *cafetières*, percolators and small espresso machines such as the Moka express pot.

A **fine grind** or filter fine grind is used for drip and filter methods.

A **fine espresso grind** is only used for espresso machines or the Neapolitan flip machines.

Powdered or **pulverized** coffee is as fine as flour and used to make strong Turkish, Greek and Arabian coffee.

Ready ground coffee is available in vacuum packs which keep the coffee fresh until the pack is opened. Finely ground coffees are packed in airtight packets. Coarser grinds, which need to give out carbon dioxide, are often contained in an airtight pack with a valve to allow the natural process to continue.

Shops which sell coffee loose will grind it for you, but there are so many good and inexpensive coffee grinders available that it is well worth grinding your own coffee at home. This enables you to grind just enough for each brewing, so that you can enjoy the coffee at its freshest before any of the flavor is lost.

When buying a coffee grinder, make sure that it is possible to adjust the grind from coarse to fine. In an electric grinder the fineness of the grind is determined by the length of time the machine is running. The results are very satisfactory, although they tend not to achieve quite the degree of fineness ideally required for Turkish coffee. Many basic manual grinders are available which are equally efficient but require more effort to operate.

Electric coffee grinder

Manual coffee grinder

Brewing Coffee

When making coffee it is important to use coffee and water in the correct proportions in order to achieve the optimum extraction from the ground coffee. Under-extraction produces a weak, sour flavor because the beans' acids are among the first substances to dissolve. Over-extraction or over-brewing also results in an unpleasant flavor. To make strong coffee it is necessary to use more coffee per cup rather than brewing the coffee for a longer time. The recommended amount of coffee is 1 to 2 tablespoons per cup. To make a weaker brew, make it at normal strength, then dilute to taste with hot water.

There are several different ways of making coffee, and a wide range of coffee-making equipment is available. However, it is generally agreed that the pot method and *cafetière* or plunger method, which are the simplest ways of making coffee, are the best.

Whichever method of coffee-making you use, follow these basic rules for good results: always keep the coffee-maker clean and warm it before use; use fresh water; never boil the coffee (with the exception of Turkish coffee); never re-use coffee grounds; avoid reheating coffee or keeping it hot for any length of time; and use plenty of good quality ground coffee.

Pot method. Heat a jug or pot and put in the required amount of coarse or medium ground coffee. Pour on hot water, leave for 2 minutes, stir, leave for another 2 minutes, then strain into cups.

Cafetière method. This is a sophisticated version of the pot method. Pour very hot water onto medium ground coffee as before. Insert the plunger into the pot, without depressing it. Let stand for a few minutes, then slowly push the plunger down so that the grounds are pushed to the bottom of the pot.

Filter method. This is another popular way of making coffee to produce an excellent brew. Although filters are now available which do not require paper filters, the finely ground coffee is usually measured into a paper filter fitted into a plastic or china cone. Individual filters may be fitted over a cup and larger ones over a coffee pot.

To make the coffee, trickle a little hot water very slowly over the finely ground coffee to allow it to swell, then pour hot water into the filter, topping it up as the water drips through. As the water drips through slowly, the pot should be kept warm on a low flame or hot plate. Electric filter machines keep the coffee hot on a thermostatically controlled hot plate, but the coffee should not be kept hot for longer than 30 minutes or it will taste stewed.

The drip pot. A cylindrical container fits over a teapot-shaped pot and the two containers are divided by a filter. Warm the pot, place the finely ground coffee in the filter, pour on the hot water and cover the upper container. When all the water has dripped through, remove the upper part, place a lid on the pot and serve.

The Neopolitan flip pot, a two-tiered coffee pot, is a variation on the drip pot. Water is boiled in the bottom half of the pot. It is then turned over to allow the boiling water to run through the coffee, which is contained in a central filter.

The percolator. In this method, steam pressure forces liquid continuously up a central tube in the pot and over the medium ground coffee. The continuous boiling ruins the taste of the coffee.

The vacuum method. Coffee freshly made by this method is excellent. Place cold water in the lower bowl. Measure the finely ground coffee into the upper filter, fix the two together and place over the heat. The water boils and rises into the upper container. When it ceases to rise, the coffee is ready.

Expresso machine or pot. This method of making coffee was invented in 1946 by Achille Gaggia. Small versions of the large com-

Coffee pot

Cafetière

mercial machines are produced for domestic use, working on the same principle. Steam and water are forced through the coffee, producing a stronger brew than is achieved simply with boiling water.

Moka espresso pots are small coffee pots which work in the same way. Fill the pot with cold water and measure the finely ground high roast coffee into the basket. Screw the pot together and heat until a gurgle indicates that the coffee is ready.

Turkish coffee. An *ibrik* or small long-handled pot is the vessel used for making Turkish coffee. It is usually made of copper or brass but, occasionally these pots are enamel. The coffee should be of a medium-high or continental roast and ground to a fine powder.

Place the coffee, sugar and water in the ibrik and bring to a boil, then remove the ibrik from the heat and stir the coffee. Repeat this process twice and serve.

Vacuum espresso coffee maker

above: Moka espresso pot

Drip pot

Coffee filter

Long-handled Turkish 'ibriks'

Espresso machine

Moka espresso pot

Espresso machine

Different methods of making coffee

Serving Coffee

Coffee can be served in a variety of ways, according to the occasion, the time of day and, above all, personal preference. However it is served, good coffee deserves to be enjoyed and appreciated, and the way to do this is to serve it very hot as soon as it is made.

It is customary to serve black coffee is small *demi-tasse* cups as an after-dinner drink. A true purist would only ever drink black coffee, but at other times of day it is quite usual to add milk or cream. *Café au lait* is the traditional French breakfast drink, made with equal quantities of coffee and hot milk and often served in a small bowl with no handles. *Café complet* is the complete French breakfast of coffee, croissant, butter and jam.

In Italy espresso is the favorite coffee, served black in small cups, sometimes with the addition of a twist of lemon peel. Steaming frothy milk is added to make cappuccino, which is often served topped with a sprinkling of powdered cinnamon or chocolate.

In Austria coffee is served in a seemingly endless variety of ways, and it is generally necessary to be quite specific as to the size of cup and exact color of coffee desired. The brew is traditionally topped with whipped cream and cinnamon or nutmeg. Sometimes the coffee will have had dried figs added, giving a thick, sweet flavor.

The combination of coffee and chocolate is universally popular. In Belgium, coffee is normally served with a small piece of chocolate which is frequently put into the cup to melt as the coffee is poured over it. Happy Marriage, a drink made of equal parts of coffee and hot chocolate, is popular in Switzerland and Germany.

Turkish and Greek coffee is served in tiny cups without handles which are placed in an outer cup made of silver or brass. It is customary for the oldest person present always to be served first.

The Arabs have a very elaborate coffee serving ritual which is comparable with the Japanese tea ceremony.

In Africa and the Middle East it is customary to add spices such as cinnamon or cardamom to coffee. Moroccans add peppercorns and the Ethiopians add a pinch of salt to their coffee.

Coffee combines well with alcohol to make an after-dinner drink and every country has a favorite combination based on the local spirit. In Normandy, for instance, generous quantities of Calvados are added to the coffee, and in Switzerland kirsch is the favorite liqueur. Rum and coffee is a popular combination, as is brandy and coffee. Perhaps the best known combination is whisky and coffee which, topped with cream, gives Gaelic coffee. Tia Maria, Kahlùa and crème de cacao also lend themselves as natural additions to coffee.

On a hot summer's day nothing is more refreshing than a glass of iced coffee. There are numerous ways of making it, sweetened or unsweetened, with or without milk or cream, but it is always essential to start off with good strong hot coffee which is allowed to cool. It can then be served in your favorite way.

Café complet: The traditional French breakfast of coffee, croissant, butter and jam. Café au lait may be preferred to black coffee.

Different ways of serving coffee

Café au lait

Cappuccino

Gaelic coffee

Belgian coffee, traditionally served with a square of chocolate

Breakfast cup of black coffee

Demi-tasse cup of coffee

Austrian coffee, topped with whipped cream and cinnamon

Coffee Additives & Substitutes

Over the years various substances have been added to or substituted for coffee, mainly for reasons of economy. To this day, many people, particularly the French, still enjoy the bitter flavor which chicory gives to coffee, and in Austria dried figs with coffee is a popular combination, called Viennese coffee. The addition of toasted barley is used in some parts of the world to make malt coffee, while toasted and ground dandelion roots are sold in health food shops as dandelion coffee. In Africa and the Middle East it is usual to enhance the flavor of the coffee with spices, and in the United States it is becoming quite fashionable to flavor coffee with vanilla or chocolate.

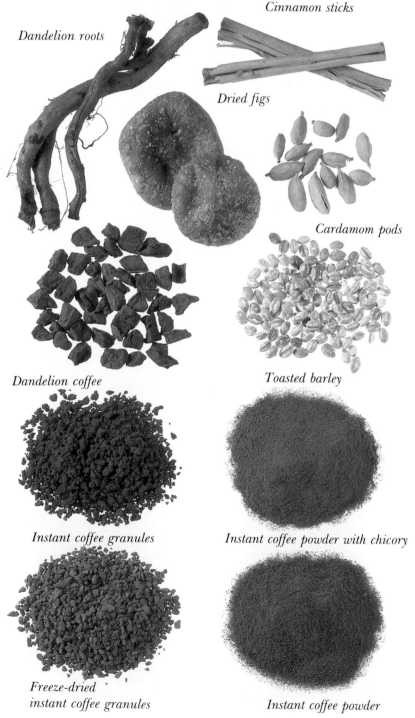

Cinnamon sticks

Dandelion roots

Dried figs

Cardamom pods

Dandelion coffee

Toasted barley

Instant coffee granules

Instant coffee powder with chicory

Freeze-dried instant coffee granules

Instant coffee powder

Instant Coffee

Instant coffee cannot compare with freshly made real coffee for aroma and flavor, but it is undeniably convenient and the better quality ones, particularly, can produce an acceptable drink which is even preferable to stale or badly made ground coffee. Instant coffee is also a useful flavoring ingredient in cooking when extra liquid is undesirable.

Most instant coffee is made from blends of medium to low grade robusta beans, but some better quality brands made from arabica beans are appearing in the shops. Instant coffee is made by brewing the coffee in large vats, then removing the water by evaporation. This is done in one of two ways.

Cheaper forms of instant coffee are spray dried to produce a fine powder. The more expensive and better quality ones are freeze-dried: water is vaporized from frozen slabs of coffee to produce coffee granules.

Instant coffee is also available as a liquid extract which is slightly sweetened and contains chicory. Coffee extract is a convenient way of adding coffee flavor in cooking.

Decaffeinated Coffee

Caffeine is one of the most commonly consumed drugs in the world, and it affects the body in a variety of ways. In small doses it has several beneficial effects, such as improving alertness, concentration and coordination, stimulating gastric secretions and causing the skeletal muscles to be less susceptible to fatigue. Taken in excess, however, it may cause over-stimulation, resulting in palpitations and insomnia in some people.

Better quality beans contain the least caffeine and robusta beans, which are mainly used for instant coffees, contain the most. This means that as the consumption of instant coffee has increased, so has the intake of caffeine. As a result, the interest in decaffeinated coffee is growing. A cup of decaffeinated coffee contains 2 to 8 mg. of caffeine, compared with 85 to 100 mg. in a cup of regular filter coffee.

Decaffeinated coffee is now widely available in bean, ground and instant forms. As technology improves, so does the quality of decaffeinated coffee. The aim is to produce a coffee which retains its aroma and flavor through the process which is necessary to remove the caffeine. As coffee develops most of its flavor during roasting, the caffeine is removed from it in its green bean form. This is done in one of three ways.

Chemical solvent decaffeination. The green beans are treated with steam to dissolve the caffeine which is then extracted, under pressure, by a chemical solvent. After decaffeination, traces of solvent are left in the coffee and these are forced out by further steaming. The coffee is then dried. Further treatment may include polishing the beans or replacing the coffee wax lost during the process.

There has been concern that the minute traces of chemicals inevitably left in the coffee beans could be harmful. However it is believed that the quantities are so negligible as to be insignificant.

Decaffeination by supercritical gas. Supercritical carbon dioxide is applied to steamed green coffee beans at high pressure and at temperatures of about 150F (70C). At this temperature the gas behaves like a liquid and is used as a solvent. The caffeine is separated from the gas by rinsing or by absorption, and the gas is recirculated. The coffee bean retains its wax layer and loses nothing but caffeine.

The Swiss water process. The green beans are soaked in water and the resulting extract is passed over activated carbon to remove the caffeine. The coffee beans are partially dried, then the caffeine-free extract is added to them before they are fully dried and roasted.

Pecan Pie

Pastry:
1-1/2 cups all-purpose flour
1/4 cup plus 3 tablespoons unsalted
  butter
1 tablespoon superfine sugar
1 egg yolk beaten with 1 tablespoon
  water

Filling:
2/3 cup maple syrup
1/2 cup light-brown sugar
3 eggs
2 tablespoons instant coffee granules
  dissolved in 1 tablespoon hot milk
1-1/2 cups pecans

Whipped cream or vanilla ice cream,
  if desired

To make pastry, sift flour into a bowl. Cut in butter until mixture resembles bread crumbs, then stir in superfine sugar. Stir in beaten egg yolk. Knead lightly to form a firm dough. Cover and chill 30 minutes.

Preheat oven to 375F (190C). On a lightly floured surface, roll out pastry and line an 8-inch flan or pie pan.

To make filling, in a saucepan, heat maple syrup and brown sugar until sugar has dissolved; cool slightly.

In a bowl, beat eggs and coffee-flavored milk; stir in maple syrup mixture and pecans. Pour into prepared pan and bake 30 to 40 minutes, until filling has set.

Serve warm or cold with whipped cream or vanilla ice cream, if desired.

Makes 6 to 8 servings.

Variation: Walnuts may be used in place of pecans and light corn syrup may be used instead of maple syrup.

Apricot Filled Crepes

Apricot Filling:
1-3/4 cups dried apricots
1/3 cup superfine sugar
2 teaspoons lemon juice
1 egg, beaten
1 tablespoon unsalted butter, softened

Coffee Crepes:
3/4 cup all-purpose flour
1 tablespoon plus 2 teaspoons
**   superfine sugar**
2 eggs, beaten
2 tablespoons instant coffee granules
**   dissolved in 2 tablespoons water**
3/4 cup plus 2 tablespoons milk
1 tablespoon unsalted butter, melted

Topping:
2 tablespoons granulated sugar
1 tablespoon unsalted butter

Coconut Cream:
1/4 cup cream of coconut
2/3 cup whipping cream

To make apricot filling, soak apricots in boiling water to cover overnight.

Transfer apricots and soaking water to a saucepan. Stir in superfine sugar. Bring to a boil, cover and sim-mer 15 minutes or until soft. Process in a blender or food processor until smooth. Stir in lemon juice and cool slightly. Stir in egg and butter; set aside.

To make crepes, sift flour into a bowl. Stir in superfine sugar, then eggs. Gradually beat in coffee, milk and butter. Let stand 1 hour.

Preheat oven to 425F (220C). Grease a 9-inch skillet.

Make 12 crepes in greased skillet. Transfer to a plate as they are cooked.

Place a spoonful of apricot filling on 1/2 of each crepe and fold in quarters. Arrange in a baking dish, sprinkle with granulated sugar and dot with butter. Bake in oven 10 to 15 minutes, until a golden crust forms on top.

To make coconut cream, in a bowl, combine cream of coconut and whipping cream; whip until just thick. Serve with crepes.

Makes 6 to 8 servings.

Babas with Kumquats

Kumquats in Syrup:
8 ozs. kumquats
2/3 cup water
1/3 cup granulated sugar

Babas:
1 cup bread flour
Pinch of salt
1 tablespoon superfine sugar
1/2 (1/4-oz.) pkg. quick-rising yeast
(1-1/2 teaspoons)
3 tablespoons milk
1/4 cup unsalted butter, softened
2 eggs, beaten

Coffee Syrup:
1/2 cup granulated sugar
2/3 cup water
1 tablespoon instant coffee granules

Slice kumquats and place in a saucepan with water. Bring to a boil, then simmer 5 minutes. Remove kumquats with a slotted spoon. Add granulated sugar to cooking water; stir until dissolved. Bring to a boil and boil steadily a few minutes, until syrup is thick and reduced by half. Return kumquats to pan; cook gently 1 minute.

To make babas, grease 8 individual 2-1/2-ounce baba pans. Sift flour and salt into a bowl; stir in sugar and yeast. Heat milk and butter to 125F to 130F (50C to 55C). Stir into dry ingredients and beat 3 to 4 minutes. Beat in eggs.

Divide mixture between prepared pans, so each one is just over half-full. Cover and let stand in a warm place 1 to 1-1/2 hours, until risen to fill pans.

Preheat oven to 400F (205C). Bake babas in oven 15 minutes, until well risen and golden.

Meanwhile, make coffee syrup. In a saucepan, heat granulated sugar and water gently until sugar is dissolved. Bring to a boil and simmer 3 minutes. Sprinkle in coffee granules and stir until dissolved.

While babas are still hot, prick with a fine skewer and spoon hot coffee syrup over them. Turn out onto individual serving plates. Reheat kumquats, if necessary, and serve with warm babas.

Makes 8 servings.

Hot Soufflé & Coffee Sabayon

Soufflé:
3 tablespoons cornstarch
1 cup milk
4 (1-oz.) squares semi-sweet chocolate,
  broken in pieces
1 tablespoon crème de cacao
4 eggs, separated
1/4 cup superfine sugar

Coffee Sabayon:
2 eggs plus 3 egg yolks
1/3 cup superfine sugar
1 tablespoon plus 1 teaspoon instant
  coffee granules
2 tablespoons dry sherry
1 tablespoon brandy

To Decorate:
Powdered sugar, if desired

Preheat oven to 375F (190C). Butter a 4-cup soufflé dish; coat with superfine sugar.

To make soufflé, in a bowl, mix cornstarch with a little milk. In a saucepan, heat remaining milk and chocolate until chocolate has melted. Pour chocolate milk into cornstarch paste, stirring constantly. Return to pan and bring to a boil, stirring constantly. Simmer 1 minute. Remove from heat and stir in crème de cacao. Stir egg yolks, 1 at a time, into mixture. Cover surface closely with plastic wrap. Cool slightly.

In a bowl, whisk egg whites until beginning to form peaks. Gradually whisk in superfine sugar until stiff but not dry; stir a little into chocolate mixture, then fold in remainder. Pour into prepared soufflé dish and bake in oven 40 minutes.

Just before soufflé is ready, make coffee sabayon. In a heavy-bottom saucepan, combine eggs and egg yolks, superfine sugar, coffee, sherry and brandy. Cook over very low heat, whisking constantly, until thick and light.

Sift powdered sugar over soufflé, if desired, and serve with sabayon.

Makes 4 to 6 servings.

Note: If using individual soufflé dishes or bake about 15 minutes.

Ginger & Coffee Soufflés

2/3 cup milk
3 tablespoons freshly ground coffee
3 tablespoons superfine sugar
Butter and granulated sugar for
    coating
2 tablespoons unsalted butter
1/4 cup all-purpose flour, sifted
3 eggs, separated
3 pieces preserved stem ginger in
    syrup, finely chopped

Crème Anglaise:
3 egg yolks
1 tablespoon plus 2 teaspoons
    superfine sugar
1-1/4 cups milk
1 tablespoon Kahlùa

To Finish:
Powdered sugar

In a saucepan, combine milk, coffee and superfine sugar. Bring to a boil, stirring constantly. Remove from heat and let stand 15 minutes to infuse.

Preheat oven to 400F (205C). Generously coat 8 (2/3-cup) ramekins with butter and granulated sugar.

In a saucepan, melt butter, then stir in flour. Strain coffee-flavored milk into mixture and stir until thick and smooth. Remove from heat and cool slightly. Stir in beaten egg yolks and ginger.

In a bowl, whisk egg whites until soft peaks form; gently fold into coffee mixture. Divide among prepared ramekins and bake in oven 15 to 20 minutes or until well risen and golden-brown.

Meanwhile, make crème anglaise. In a bowl, whisk egg yolks and superfine sugar until thick and light. In a saucepan, bring milk to a boil. Slowly stir into egg yolks, then strain back into pan. Cook over a very low heat, stirring constantly, until mixture thickens. Stir in Kahlùa.

Sprinkle soufflés with powdered sugar and serve immediately with crème anglaise.

Makes 8 servings.

Baked Apricots

1 cup large dried apricots (about 18)
1 pot freshly made Earl Grey tea
3/4 cup ground almonds
1/3 cup powdered sugar, sifted
1/4 cup unsalted butter, melted
1 tablespoon lemon juice
18 blanched almonds
2 teaspoons sweet sherry
Chilled yogurt, if desired

Put apricots into a bowl. Strain hot tea over them and soak overnight.

Preheat oven to 400F (205C).

In a bowl, mix ground almonds, powdered sugar, all but 2 teaspoons of melted butter and lemon juice. Knead to a smooth paste.

Drain apricots; pat dry with paper towels.

Divide almond paste in 18 pieces; press each piece around an almond and use to stuff apricots.

Brush a baking dish with remaining butter. Put apricots into dish and sprinkle with sherry. Cover with buttered waxed paper and bake in oven 10 minutes.

Serve hot with yogurt, if desired.

Makes 6 servings.

Variations: Prunes or dried peaches may be used instead of apricots.

Different flavors of tea may be used to soak fruit.

Strawberry Tea Ice Cream

4 strawberry-flavored tea bags
1-1/4 cups boiling water
2 eggs, separated, plus 4 yolks
1 cup superfine sugar
1-1/4 cups milk
1-1/4 cups whipping cream

Caramel Strawberries:
3/4 cup superfine sugar
1/4 cup water
Pinch of cream of tartar
12 to 18 strawberries with stems

Put tea bags into a saucepan. Pour over boiling water and let stand 5 minutes to infuse.

In a bowl, whisk 6 yolks and superfine sugar until thick and light.

Remove tea bags from pan. Add milk and bring to a boil. Slowly stir into egg yolk mixture, then pour mixture into pan. Heat gently, stirring constantly with a wooden spoon, until mixture thickens and coats back of spoon. Strain into a bowl and cool.

In another bowl, whip cream until soft peaks form; fold into custard. Freeze until mixture is slushy, then beat thoroughly. In a separate bowl, whisk egg whites until soft peaks form; fold into ice cream. Transfer to a freezerproof container. Cover, seal and freeze about 3 hours, until firm.

To make caramel strawberries, grease a baking sheet. Put sugar and water into a saucepan and heat gently until sugar has dissolved. Add cream of tartar. Bring to a boil and boil syrup to 300F (150C) or until a drop of syrup hardens when dropped into a cup of cold water. Remove from heat. Dip strawberries into caramel and put on greased baking sheet to harden.

Remove ice cream from freezer 30 minutes before serving to soften. Scoop onto chilled serving plates and decorate with strawberries.

Makes 6 servings.

Note: The caramelized strawberries should be eaten within 30 minutes, otherwise they begin to soften.

Earl Grey Sorbet

1-3/4 cups plus 2 tablespoons freshly
made Earl Grey tea
1 lemon
Mint leaves
1/3 cup superfine sugar
2/3 cup white wine
2 egg whites

Spun Sugar:
3/4 cup granulated sugar
2/3 cup water

Strain tea into a bowl. Pare a few strips of peel from lemon; add to tea with mint. Add superfine sugar, stirring until dissolved. Let stand until cold, then stir in wine. Pour into a freezerproof container. Cover, seal and freeze 1 to 1-1/2 hours, until mushy.

In a food processor, process sorbet to break up ice crystals. In a bowl, whisk egg whites until soft peaks form. Add to sorbet in food processor and process until well blended. Return mixture to freezer.

Freeze 1 hour, then process in food processor. Repeat, then freeze 2 hours, until firm.

To make spun sugar, cover floor of work area with newspaper. Suspend handle of a wooden spoon over newspaper covered area.

Put granulated sugar and water into a saucepan and heat gently until sugar has dissolved. Bring to a boil and boil rapidly, without stirring, to 305F (155C) or until a drop of syrup hardens immediately when dropped into a cup of cold water. Using 2 large forks and working quickly, dip forks lightly into toffee. Wave over spoon handle so toffee is thrown in very fine threads and hangs over handle.

Gather up spun sugar. Keep in a cold dry place up to 6 hours.

Scoop sorbet onto chilled serving plates and decorate with spun sugar to serve.

Makes 6 servings.

Note: As an alternative to spun sugar, serve this delicate sorbet with wafer cookies.

Praline Coffee Ice Cream

Praline:
1/3 cup blanched almonds
1/4 cup superfine sugar

3 egg yolks
1/3 cup granulated sugar
1/2 cup water
2 cups whipping cream
2 tablespoons instant coffee granules dissolved in 1 tablespoon plus 1 teaspoon hot water
1 tablespoon Kahlùa

To make praline, oil a baking sheet. In a heavy-bottom saucepan, gently heat almonds and superfine sugar, stirring frequently, until sugar has dissolved. Cook, stirring constantly, until rich golden-brown. Turn onto prepared baking sheet and let stand until completely cold and hard. Crush with a rolling pin or in a food processor. Set aside.

In a bowl, beat egg yolks until light and thick; set aside. In a saucepan, heat granulated sugar and water until sugar has dissolved. Increase heat and boil rapidly to thread stage (230F/110C). To test, dip fingers into cold water. Take a little syrup with a spoon then pull apart betwen thumb and forefinger. Syrup is ready when a 1-inch long thread of syrup forms. Cool 1 minute.

Pour syrup into beaten egg yolks, whisking until mixture is thick and mousse-like. In a bowl, whip cream until light, but not thick. Stir in cooled coffee and Kahlùa. Fold coffee cream into egg yolk mixture. Stir in praline.

Pour mixture into a 4-cup container. Freeze until mixture is half frozen, then transfer to a bowl and whisk. Return to freezer until firm.

Transfer ice cream to refrigerator 30 minutes before serving to soften. Scoop into chilled glass dishes to serve.

Makes 6 servings.

Granita di Caffe

3/4 cup superfine sugar
1-1/4 cups water
3-3/4 cups hot strong coffee

To Serve:
2/3 cup whipping cream
2 teaspoons powdered sugar, sifted
2 teaspoons Tia Maria
Crisp dessert cookies

To Decorate:
12 to 16 coffee beans

In a saucepan, combine sugar and water. Stir over low heat until sugar has dissolved. Bring to a boil. Boil rapidly 5 minutes; cool.

Strain coffee through coffee filter paper or a sieve lined with paper towels into sugar syrup and mix. Pour into a 4-cup freezerproof container and freeze 3 hours or until granular, stirring occasionally.

In a bowl, whip cream and powdered sugar until fairly stiff. Stir in Tia Maria.

Spoon granita into sorbet cups or glasses and top with flavored cream and coffee beans. Serve with crisp dessert cookies.

Makes 6 to 8 servings.

Note: Granita should be coarse and granular, not smooth like a sorbet. If it is removed from the freezer and later replaced once it has begun to thaw, the characteristic texture will be lost.

Variations: To make granita into iced coffee, stir 2/3 cup whipping cream into frozen granita.

Strawberry Granita: Replace coffee with puree made from 2 pounds of strawberries and juice of 1 lemon. Use half quantity of sugar.

Lemon Granita: Use half quantity of sugar and 2-1/2 cups of water. Replace coffee with 1-1/4 cups of lemon juice and grated peel of lemon.

Kulfi & Coriander Curls

Kulfi:
1 tablespoon cornstarch
5 cups milk
5 cardamom pods
1/4 cup superfine sugar
2 tablespoons finely ground coffee
1/2 cup ground almonds

Coriander Curls:
1 egg white
1/4 cup superfine sugar
1/4 cup all-purpose flour, sifted
1 teaspoon ground coriander
Grated peel of 1/2 orange
2 tablespoons unsalted butter, melted

To make kulfi, mix cornstarch with 1 tablespoon of milk; set aside. Put remaining milk and cardamom pods into a saucepan. Bring to a boil and boil gently about 1 hour, until milk is reduced to 2-1/2 cups. Strain into a bowl. Stir in superfine sugar and coffee and let stand 5 minutes.

Wash pan. Strain milk through a fine sieve back into pan. Stir in blended cornstarch and cook, stirring constantly, until mixture thickens slightly. Remove from heat, stir in ground almonds and let stand until cold. Freeze in ice cube trays about 1 hour, until firm.

To make coriander curls, preheat oven to 375F (190C). Grease 4 to 5 baking sheets.

In a bowl, beat egg white and superfine sugar. Stir in flour, coriander, orange peel and butter. Drop 3 to 4 teaspoonfuls of mixture, spacing well apart, on each prepared baking sheet; mixture will make approximately 16 curls. Bake in oven 6 minutes or until pale golden-brown.

Remove cookies from baking sheets and curl around a rolling pin; cool.

Turn ice cream cubes out onto individual serving plates and serve with curls.

Makes 4 servings.

Note: Bake cookies 1 sheet at a time or they will harden before you have time to roll them.

If desired, kulfi may be frozen in individual freezerproof ramekins.

Iced Coffee Soufflés

4 eggs, separated
1/2 cup superfine sugar
1 tablespoon instant coffee granules
1 tablespoon Tia Maria
1-1/4 cups whipping cream

Passion Fruit Sauce:
4 to 5 passion fruit
1/4 cup superfine sugar
1 tablespoon cornstarch
1 cup water

To Decorate:
Sprigs of mint

In a bowl, whisk egg yolks and 1/3 cup of sugar. Put bowl over a pan of hot water and continue whisking until mixture thickens. Add coffee granules and stir until dissolved. Stir in Tia Maria; cool.

In a bowl, whip cream until soft peaks form; fold into coffee mixture. In a clean bowl, whisk egg whites and remaining sugar until soft peaks form; fold into mixture.

Spoon into 6 to 8 freezerproof ramekin dishes. Cover, seal and freeze about 4 hours, until firm.

To make sauce, cut passion fruit in half and scoop out pulp into a bowl. Put superfine sugar, cornstarch and water into a saucepan and cook gently, stirring constantly, until beginning to thicken. Stir in passion fruit pulp and cook 2 minutes. Strain into a bowl, stir in a few passion fruit seeds and cool.

To serve, dip ramekins into hot water and turn soufflés out onto serving dishes. Place in refrigerator 15 minutes to soften. Decorate soufflés with mint sprigs and serve with sauce.

Makes 6 to 8 servings.

Variation: Tape waxed paper collars around 6 small ramekins. Fill with soufflé mixture to come above top of ramekins. Freeze until firm. Remove waxed paper collars before serving.

Chestnut & Coffee Bombe

Chestnut Ice Cream:
3 eggs, separated
1/3 cup superfine sugar
1/2 cup unsweetened chestnut puree
2 tablespooons brandy
1-1/4 cups whipping cream

Coffee Sorbet:
1/4 cup superfine sugar
1-1/4 cups water
3 tablespoons finely ground coffee
1/2 egg white

To Decorate:
Chocolate leaves, see page 86

To make chestnut ice cream, in a bowl, whisk egg yolks and superfine sugar until thick and light. In another bowl, mix chestnut puree and brandy until smooth.

In a third bowl, whip cream until just holding its shape. Fold chestnut puree into egg yolk mixture, then fold in whipped cream. In a clean bowl, whisk egg whites until soft peaks form; fold into mixture.

Pour mixture into a freezerproof container and freeze 1-1/2 to 2 hours, until nearly firm, stirring twice. Turn into a chilled 5-cup bombe mold or bowl and press around bottom and side. Return to freezer.

To make coffee sorbet, put sugar and water into a saucepan and heat gently, stirring constantly, until sugar has dissolved. Bring to a boil and boil 4 minutes. Stir in ground coffee, remove from heat and let stand 10 minutes to infuse. Pour through a fine sieve into a freezerproof container. Cool, then freeze 1 to 1-1/2 hours, until slushy. Transfer to a bowl.

In a bowl, beat egg white until soft peaks form; beat into coffee mixture. Pour into center of bombe mold and freeze about 2 hours, until firm.

Transfer to refrigerator 30 minutes before serving to soften. Turn out onto a serving plate and decorate with chocolate leaves.

Makes 8 servings.

Jamaican Layer Ice Cream

Coffee Ice Cream:
1-1/4 cups half and half
1/3 cup freshly ground coffee
4 egg yolks
2/3 cup superfine sugar
1-1/4 cups whipping cream, whipped

Pineapple Ice Cream:
1/2 pineapple, peeled, cored
1 egg white
1/4 cup superfine sugar
2 tablespoons white rum
2/3 cup whipping cream, whipped

To Decorate:
Pineapple pieces

To make coffee ice cream, in a saucepan, heat half and half almost to boiling point. Add ground coffee, stir well and let stand 30 minutes.

In a bowl, whisk egg yolks and superfine sugar until thick and light. Reheat coffee-flavored cream until almost boiling. Strain through cheesecloth into egg yolk mixture. Set bowl over a pan of hot water and cook, stirring constantly, until mixture thickens. Cool, then fold in whipped cream.

Line a 9" x 5" x 3" loaf pan with plastic wrap. Spread 1/2 of coffee mixture in bottom of pan. Cover and freeze about 2 hours, until half-frozen. Set aside remaining coffee custard.

To make pineapple ice cream, in a blender or food processor, process pineapple to a puree. In a bowl, whisk egg white until soft peaks form. Gradually whisk in superfine sugar. Fold into pineapple puree with rum. Fold in whipped cream.

Spread over coffee ice cream in pan. Cover and freeze about 2 hours, until firm; freeze remaining coffee custard at same time. Stir coffee ice cream to soften slightly, spread over pineapple ice cream and return to freezer about 2 hours, until firm.

Turn out onto a serving plate and place in refrigerator 20 minutes before serving to soften. Serve in slices, decorated with pineapple pieces.

Makes 8 servings.

Amaretti Semifreddo

12 pairs amaretti cookies
1-3/4 cups plus 2 tablespoons
    whipping cream
2 tablespoons instant coffee granules
    dissolved in 1 tablespoon hot water
1 cup powdered sugar, sifted
4 egg whites
2 (1-oz.) squares semi-sweet chocolate

Crush amaretti cookies with a rolling pin or in a food processor.

In a bowl, mix whipping cream and cooled coffee, then stir in powdered sugar. Whip until beginning to thicken. Stir in crushed cookies.

In a bowl, whisk egg whites until soft peaks form; carefully fold into amaretti mixture. Transfer to a long narrow freezerproof container. Cover, seal and freeze about 2 hours, until quite firm.

Turn ice cream out onto a sheet of foil or plastic wrap and, using foil or plastic wrap as a guide, shape in a log. Wrap up firmly and return to freezer 2 to 3 hours, until firm.

Grate chocolate finely onto a flat surface. Unwrap ice cream. Roll ice cream in grated chocolate to coat completely. Keep in freezer until required. Serve cut in slices.

Makes 6 to 8 servings.

Note: If you do not have a long narrow container, freeze ice cream in 2 small loaf pans. Place side by side on foil to shape in a log.

This type of ice cream never sets completely solid so it is not necessary to soften before serving.

Variation: Stir grated chocolate into ice cream mixture and roll log in crushed amaretti cookies to coat.

Coffee Parfait

1/2 cup superfine sugar
2/3 cup water
3 eggs
1 tablespoon plus 1 teaspoon instant
   coffee granules dissolved in 1
   tablespoon boiling water
2/3 cup whipping cream

Chocolate Cups:
4 (1-oz.) squares semi-sweet chocolate,
   broken in pieces

To Decorate:
Chocolate leaves, see page 86

Put sugar and water into a saucepan and heat until sugar has dissolved. Bring to a boil and boil steadily to 230F (110C) or until a little of syrup forms a thread when pressed between a wet thumb and forefinger when drawn apart.

In a bowl set over a pan of simmering water, whisk eggs until frothy. Pour syrup onto eggs and whisk, still over simmering water, until mixture is pale and thick and whisk leaves a trail when lifted. Stir in coffee. Remove from heat and set over a bowl of iced water. Whisk mixture until cool.

In another bowl, whip cream until just beginning to hold its shape; fold into coffee mixture. Turn into a freezerproof container. Cover, seal and freeze 2 to 3 hours, until firm.

To make chocolate cups, melt chocolate in a bowl set over a pan of hot water. Cool slightly. Spread melted chocolate evenly inside 12 to 16 double thickness of paper baking cups with a brush or spoon, coating bottom and side. Let stand until set. Add another layer of chocolate, if necessary. When set, carefully peel away paper cups.

Remove parfait from freezer 10 minutes before serving to soften. Scoop into chocolate cups and decorate with chocolate leaves.

Makes 6 to 8 servings.

Rose Petal Tea Cream

Crystallized Rose Petals:
20 clean dry unblemished rose petals
1 egg white, lightly beaten
Superfine sugar

2 tablespoons rose pouchong tea
1-1/4 cups milk
2 eggs, separated
1/4 cup superfine sugar
1 teaspoon rose water
1 (1/4-oz.) pkg. unflavored gelatin
   (1 tablespoon)
3 tablespoons water
2/3 cup whipping cream
Crisp cookies or grapes, if desired

To make crystallized rose petals, brush petals with egg white. Gently toss in superfine sugar until completely coated. Let stand on a wire rack in a warm dry place until dry.

In a saucepan, bring tea and milk to a boil. Remove from heat and let stand 5 minutes to infuse.

In a bowl, whisk egg yolks and superfine sugar. Strain tea-flavored milk into egg yolk mixture; stir in rose water.

Dissolve gelatin in water; stir into tea mixture. Chill until just beginning to set.

In a bowl, whip cream; fold into tea mixture.

In a clean bowl, whisk egg white until soft peaks form; gently fold into tea mixture. Turn into 4 wetted (3/4-cup) individual molds and chill 2 to 3 hours, until set.

Turn out onto individual serving plates. Decorate with crystallized rose petals and serve with crisp cookies or grapes, if desired.

Makes 4 servings.

Mocha Mousse in Filo Cups

3 sheets filo pastry
1 tablespoon unsalted butter, melted

Mousse:
4 (1-oz.) squares semi-sweet chocolate,
  broken in pieces
1 tablespoon plus 1 teaspoon instant
  coffee granules dissolved in 2
  tablespoons water
2 eggs, separated
2/3 cup whipping cream

To Decorate:
Powdered sugar

Preheat oven to 375F (190C). Cut each sheet of filo pastry in 12 (3-inch) squares.

Put a square of pastry in each of 12 cups of a muffin pan. Lightly brush pastry with butter. Put another square diagonally on top; brush with butter. Cover with a third square of pastry; brush with butter. Press a square of foil into each pastry cup and bake in oven 10 minutes or until pas-

try is crisp and golden. Cool on a wire rack.

To make mousse, put chocolate and cold coffee in a bowl set over a pan of hot water and let stand until chocolate has melted. Stir until smooth, then stir in egg yolks.

In a bowl, whip cream until soft peaks form. Fold whipped cream into chocolate mixture.

In a clean bowl, whisk egg whites until soft peaks form. Fold into chocolate mixture. Let stand until slightly thickened, then spoon into filo cups. Chill 15 minutes.

Sprinkle with powdered sugar before serving.

Makes 6 servings.

Note: Do not leave mousse in filo cups more than 30 minutes before serving as pastry softens quickly.

Coffee & Cardamom Caramel

10 cardamom pods
2-1/2 cups milk
2 eggs
2 egg yolks
2 tablespoons plus 2 teaspoons
  superfine sugar
2 tablespoons instant coffee granules

Caramel:
1/2 cup granulated sugar
1/4 cup water

Preheat oven to 325F (160C).

Lightly crush cardamom pods and place in a saucepan with milk. Heat almost to boiling point, then remove from heat and set aside.

To make caramel, place granulated sugar and water in a heavy-bottom saucepan. Heat gently until sugar has dissolved, then bring to a boil and boil rapidly until syrup turns a light golden-brown. Pour into 6 (2/3-cup) ramekin dishes and set aside.

In a large bowl, beat eggs and egg yolks lightly. Stir in superfine sugar. Reheat milk until almost boiling. Add coffee and stir until dissolved. Slowly stir coffee-flavored milk into egg and sugar mixture.

Strain custard into a bowl, then carefully pour it into ramekins on top of caramel. Place ramekins in a roasting pan and pour in enough hot water to come halfway up side of ramekins. Bake in oven about 45 minutes or until set; test by inserting a knife into custard—it should leave a clean cut.

Remove ramekins from pan and cool. Chill well before turning out into individual dishes.

Makes 6 servings.

Note: Cardamom imparts a superb flavor, but pods must be as fresh as possible to ensure a good result.

Vanilla & Coffee Bavarois

4 egg yolks
1/4 cup superfine sugar
1-1/4 cups milk
1 vanilla bean
1 (1/4-oz.) pkg. unflavored gelatin
  (1 tablespoon)
1 tablespoon strong coffee
Few drops vanilla extract
1-1/4 cups whipping cream

Coffee Sauce:
2/3 cup half and half
1 tablespoon strong coffee
1 teaspoon instant coffee granules

Lightly oil 6 (2/3-cup) molds.

In a bowl, whisk egg yolks and sugar until thick and pale.

In a saucepan, bring milk and vanilla pod slowly to a boil. Remove vanilla pod; slowly pour milk over egg yolk mixture, stirring well. Place over a pan of hot, but not boiling, water. Stir frequently until custard has thickened and coats back of a spoon. Sprinkle gelatin into mixture, whisking well. When gelatin has dissolved, strain custard equally into 2 bowls. Stir coffee into 1 bowl and vanilla extract into other. Cover surface of custard closely with plastic wrap; cool.

When mixtures are on point of setting, whip cream lightly; fold 1/2 of whipped cream into each bowl. Divide coffee custard among oiled molds. Cover with vanilla custard. Chill at least 3 hours or until set.

To serve, invert molds onto serving plates.

To make sauce, in a bowl, combine all but 2 tablespoons of half and half with coffee; pour around molds. Carefully pour reserved cream in a thin line around sauce and feather into a design, using a skewer. Sprinkle with coffee granules just before serving.

Makes 6 servings.

Floating Islands

Coffee Custard:
4 egg yolks
2 tablespoons plus 2 teaspoons
superfine sugar
1-3/4 cups milk
2 tablespoons strong coffee

Meringues:
4 egg whites
2/3 cup superfine sugar

To Decorate:
2 tablespoons grated semi-sweet
chocolate

To make custard, in a bowl, beat egg yolks and sugar. In a saucepan, heat milk to just below boiling point. Slowly pour into egg yolks, stirring constantly. Strain back into rinsed pan. Stir over low heat until custard thickens and coats back of spoon. *It must not boil.* Stir in coffee. Cool, stirring occasionally to prevent a skin from forming.

To make meringues, in a bowl, whisk egg whites until stiff. Gradually whisk in 1/2 of superfine sugar. Fold in remaining superfine sugar with a large metal spoon. Bring a large skillet of water to simmering point. Drop 4 heaping tablespoonfuls of meringue into water, spacing well apart. Simmer 3 to 4 minutes. Turn with a slotted spoon and simmer 2 to 3 minutes more. Remove from water and drain on paper towels.

Repeat until all meringue mixture is used. Mixture should make 18 meringues. Cool.

To serve, divide coffee custard among 6 individual plates. Arrange 3 meringues on each pool of sauce and sprinkle with grated chocolate.

Makes 6 servings.

Meringues with Caramel & Lime

2 egg whites
1/2 cup superfine sugar
1 tablespoon plus 1 teaspoon instant
   coffee granules

Caramel-Lime Sauce:
1/2 cup granulated sugar
1/2 cup water
1 lime

To Finish:
2/3 cup whipping cream

Preheat oven to 250F (120C). Line 2 baking sheets with parchment paper.

In a bowl, whisk egg whites until stiff. Gradually whisk in 1/2 of superfine sugar. Fold in remaining superfine sugar and coffee granules.

Spoon into a pastry bag fitted with a 1/4-inch nozzle and pipe 36 heart shapes onto prepared baking sheets. Bake in oven 1-1/2 hours or until completely dry; cool.

To make caramel-lime sauce, heat granulated sugar and 1/4 cup of water gently in a saucepan until sugar has dissolved. Increase heat and cook until syrup turns deep golden. Remove from heat and carefully add remaining water.

Thinly pare peel from lime. Cut in fine shreds and set aside. Squeeze juice from 1/2 of lime and add to prepared caramel; cool.

In a bowl, whip cream until thick. Spoon into a pastry bag fitted with a fluted nozzle. Sandwich meringues together in pairs with piped cream, placing bottom meringue flat side down.

Arrange 3 meringues on each plate and pour sauce around. Pipe a cream rosette on each meringue and decorate with lime peel shreds.

Makes 6 servings.

Coffee Gelatin with Mango

Gelatin:
3/4 cup superfine sugar
1/3 cup water
2 (1/4-oz.) pkgs. unflavored gelatin
(2 tablespoons)
3-3/4 cups hot strong coffee

Mango Filling:
2 ripe mangos
2/3 cup crème fraîche
1 passion fruit

In a saucepan, dissolve sugar in water over low heat. Bring to a boil and boil steadily 2 minutes.

Sprinkle gelatin over hot coffee. When dissolved, whisk in thoroughly. Stir in sugar syrup. Strain through a sieve lined with paper towels into a bowl. Cool, then pour into 4 wetted (3/4-cup) individual molds. Chill in refrigerator until set.

To make mango filling, peel man-gos, then cut flesh away from pit. Cut 1/2 of 1 mango into slices and set aside.

In a blender or food processor, puree remaining mango flesh. In a bowl, mix mango puree and crème fraîche.

To serve, dip molds briefly into hot water and turn out onto individual serving plates. Pour mango cream around molds and decorate with re-served mango slices. Cut passion fruit in half and scoop out flesh and seeds. Sprinkle over mango cream.

Makes 4 servings.

Note: To ensure that gelatin is as clear as possible, individual molds must be absolutely clean and free from grease before they are used.

Pear-Amaretto Custard

Poached Pears:
1/2 cup granulated sugar
1-1/4 cups water
1/4 cup maple syrup
2 firm cooking pears

Caramel:
1/2 cup superfine sugar
2 tablespoons water

12 pairs amaretti cookies
2-1/2 cups milk
2 tablespoons instant coffee granules
1/4 cup superfine sugar
4 eggs, beaten
2 tablespoons rum
1 tablespoon amaretto liqueur

To prepare pears, put granulated sugar and water into a saucepan and heat gently until sugar has dissolved. Bring to a boil and boil 5 minutes. Add maple syrup. Peel pears and cut lengthwise in slices. Add to syrup and cook gently about 10 minutes, depending upon ripeness, until soft; cool.

Preheat oven to 350F (175C).

To make caramel, put sugar and water into a saucepan and heat gently until sugar has dissolved. Bring to a boil and boil to a golden caramel. Pour into 8 individual ramekins, tipping to coat sides completely; set aside.

Crush amaretti cookies and put into a bowl. In a saucepan, heat milk until almost boiling; stir in coffee granules. Pour over cookie crumbs and let stand a few minutes, until crumbs are soft. Stir well to blend with milk, then stir in superfine sugar, eggs, rum and amaretto liqueur. Divide among ramekins.

Place ramekins in a baking dish containing enough hot water to come halfway up sides. Bake in oven 30 minutes or until a knife inserted into each custard comes out clean. Let stand until cold, then chill 2 hours. Turn out onto individual serving plates and decorate with pear slices.

Makes 8 servings.

Note: Use traditional Italian amaretti cookies sold tissue-wrapped in pairs.

Coffee Syllabub & Brandy Snaps

6 gingersnap cookies, crushed

Syllabub:
1/2 cup strong coffee
1 tablespoon brandy
1 tablespoon Tia Maria
1/4 cup superfine sugar
Pinch of grated nutmeg
1-1/4 cups whipping cream

Brandy Snaps:
1 tablespoon light corn syrup
2 tablespoons superfine sugar
2 tablespoons butter
3 tablespoons all-purpose flour
1/2 teaspoon ground ginger
1 teaspoon brandy

Divide cookie crumbs between 6 syllabub cups or tall glasses, reserving some for decoration.

To make syllabub, in a bowl, mix coffee, brandy, Tia Maria, sugar and nutmeg. Stir until sugar has dissolved. Whisk in cream until mixture thickens and holds soft peaks. Spoon over cookie crumbs. Refrigerate several hours or overnight, if desired.

To make brandy snaps, preheat oven to 350F (175C). Lightly grease 2 baking sheets.

In a heavy-bottom saucepan, slowly warm syrup, sugar and butter until sugar has dissolved and mixture is smooth. Remove from heat and sift in flour and ginger. Beat into mixture with brandy. Drop 18 half-teaspoonfuls of mixture onto baking sheets, allowing room for spreading. Bake in oven 10 minutes or until golden and lacy.

Remove from oven and cool 1 to 2 minutes. Remove brandy snaps from baking sheets and quickly roll each one around a thin stick (a chopstick is ideal). If they start to harden before rolling, return to oven 1 to 2 minutes. Let stand 1 to 2 minutes to set, then remove stick and transfer brandy snaps to a wire rack to cool.

Sprinkle reserved cookie crumbs on top of syllabubs. Serve with brandy snaps.

Makes 6 servings.

Charlotte Malakoff

1/2 cup unsalted butter, softened
1/2 cup superfine sugar
1 egg yolk
1/2 cup ground walnuts
1/2 cup ground almonds
1/3 cup strong coffee
2/3 cup whipping cream
1 tablespoon Tia Maria
3 ladyfinger cookies

To Decorate:
Chocolate leaves, see page 86

Line a 9" x 5" x 3" loaf pan with plastic wrap.

In a bowl, cream butter and sugar until light and fluffy. Add egg yolk, ground nuts and 2 tablespoons of coffee.

In a bowl, whip cream; fold 3 tablespoons into nut mixture. Cover remaining cream and refrigerate.

In a shallow dish, mix remaining coffee and Tia Maria. Quickly dip in ladyfingers, then arrange a layer to cover bottom of prepared pan. Spread 1/2 of nut and coffee cream over ladyfingers. Cover with layer of ladyfingers. Spread with remaining nut and coffee cream. Finish with a layer of ladyfingers. Chill several hours or overnight.

Turn out onto a plate. Spread reserved cream over top and decorate with chocolate leaves.

Makes 8 servings.

Chocolate & Coffee Wafers

Crème Anglaise:
1-1/4 cups milk
1 vanilla bean
3 egg yolks
1 tablespoon plus 2 teaspoons
   superfine sugar

6 (1-oz.) squares semi-sweet chocolate,
   melted
1-1/4 cups whipping cream
1 tablespoon plus 1 teaspoon instant
   coffee granules
2 tablespoons boiling water
1/2 (1/4-oz.) pkg. unflavored gelatin
   (1-1/2 teaspoons)
1 tablespoon Tia Maria
2 egg yolks
1/4 cup superfine sugar

To Decorate:
1 tablespoon coarsely chopped
   pistachios

To make crème angliase, put milk and vanilla pod in a saucepan; bring almost to boiling point. Remove vanilla pod. In a bowl, slowly whisk egg yolks and sugar until thick and light; whisk in hot milk. Return to pan and cook over very low heat, stirring constantly, until mixture thickens slightly. Strain into a bowl, cover with a tea towel and cool. Meanwhile, make wafers.

Cut 6 (2-1/2" x 10-1/2") strips of parchment paper. Brush evenly with melted chocolate. Mark each strip with a knife every 3-1/2 inches. Refrigerate until set. Carefully peel off chocolate wafers.

In a bowl, whip cream. In another bowl, mix coffee granules and boiling water; sprinkle with gelatin and as gelatin dissolves, stir in coffee. Stir in Tia Maria. In another bowl, whisk egg yolks and sugar until thick and light. Stir in coffee. Fold in whipped cream. Refrigerate until just beginning to set.

Spoon mousse mixture into a pastry bag. Arrange 6 chocolate wafers on a tray and pipe with mousse. Lay a second wafer on top and pipe with another layer of mousse. Top with a final chocolate wafer.

Pour crème anglaise onto 6 plates. Arrange a wafer in center and pipe a line of mousse on top. Sprinkle pistachios over sauce.

Makes 6 servings.

Moroccan Fruit Compote

2 peach-flavored tea bags
5 cups boiling water
1 cup dried apricots
3/4 cup dried peaches
2/3 cup pitted prunes
1/3 cup raisins
1/3 cup sugar
1/3 cup blanched whole almonds
1/2 cup pistachios
1 pomegranate, if desired
Plain yogurt, if desired

Shortbread:
1/4 cup unsalted butter, softened
1 tablespoon plus 2 teaspoons
   superfine sugar
1 teaspoon rose water
3/4 cup all-purpose flour, sifted
12 blanched whole almonds

Put tea bags into a bowl. Pour over boiling water and let stand 5 minutes to infuse. Remove tea bags. Add apricots, peaches, prunes and raisins to tea and soak overnight.

In a saucepan, combine fruit, soaking liquid and granulated sugar. Bring to a boil, then simmer gently 15 to 20 minutes, until fruit is soft. Add almonds and pistachio nuts. Transfer to a serving dish and cool.

To make shortbread, preheat oven to 375F (190C). In a bowl, cream butter, superfine sugar and rose water until light and fluffy. Stir in flour, then mix to a firm dough; divide in 12 pieces. Roll each piece in a ball and place on a baking sheet. Press an almond onto each ball. Bake in oven 10 minutes, until golden. Transfer to a wire rack to cool.

If desired, cut pomegranate in half, scoop out seeds and stir into compote. Serve compote with yogurt, if desired, and shortbread.

Makes 6 servings.

Almond & Coffee Tartlets

Pastry:
1 cup all-purpose flour
1/3 cup ground almonds
1/4 cup plus 2 tablespoons butter,
   softened
1 tablespoon plus 2 teaspoons
   superfine sugar
1 egg yolk
1 tablespoon cold water

Filling:
2 egg yolks
Pinch salt
2 teaspoons superfine sugar
3/4 cup almond oil
1 teaspoon instant coffee granules
   dissolved in 1 tablespoon hot water
1 teaspoon brandy

To Decorate:
1 tablespoon sliced almonds, toasted
Semi-sweet chocolate, melted

To make pastry, sift flour onto a flat surface. Mix in ground almonds. Make a well in center and add butter, superfine sugar, egg yolk and cold water. Using fingertips of 1 hand, pinch ingredients together until well blended. Gradually work in flour and ground almonds until mixture forms a smooth pliable dough. Wrap in plastic wrap and chill 1 hour.

Preheat oven to 375F (190C).

On a lightly floured surface, roll out pastry thinly and line 12 tartlet pans; prick bottoms. Press a square of foil firmly into each tartlet. Bake in oven 10 minutes. Remove foil and bake 10 minutes more or until pastry is golden and firm to touch. Cool on a wire rack.

To make filling, in a bowl, whisk egg yolks, salt and sugar. Gradually add oil, beating constantly. As mixture thickens, add coffee and brandy. Divide mixture among tartlet shells. Sprinkle with almonds and drizzle with chocolate.

Makes 12 servings.

Variations: Replace almonds with chocolate curls or fruit such as blackberries, raspberries or cherries.

Caramel & Coffee Profiteroles

Choux Pastry:
2/3 cup bread flour
1/4 cup butter
2/3 cup water
2 eggs, beaten

Coffee Crème Pâtissière:
4 eggs, separated
1/4 cup superfine sugar
1/4 cup all-purpose flour
1-1/4 cups milk
1 teaspoon strong coffee
1 tablespoon plus 1 teaspoon
   whipping cream, whipped

Caramel Topping:
1/2 cup granulated sugar
1/4 cup water
1/4 cup hazelnuts, coarsely chopped,
   toasted

Preheat oven to 425F (220C).

To make choux pastry, sift flour onto a sheet of waxed paper. In a saucepan, gently heat butter and water until butter has melted, then bring to a boil. When boiling, add salt and flour all at once. Beat with a wooden spoon 1 minute until mixture forms a ball and leaves side of pan clean. Allow to cool a little.

Add eggs to mixture a little at a time, beating thoroughly. Mixture should be smooth and glossy and able to hold its own shape. Add a little more egg if necessary.

Drop teaspoonfuls of mixture onto dampened baking sheets. Bake in oven 10 minutes. Lower heat to 375F (190C) and bake 20 to 25 minutes more or until golden and crisp. Make a slit in side of each bun. Cool on wire racks.

Make and cool crème pâtissière, following directions on page 85. Fold in whipped cream. Fill choux buns with cold crème patissiere.

To make topping, in a small saucepan, gently heat granulated sugar and water until sugar has dissolved. Increase heat and cook rapidly until mixture is light golden-brown. Coat top of each bun with caramel. Quickly sprinkle with nuts. When caramel is hard, pile buns up in a serving dish. Serve within 2 hours.

Makes 20 buns.

Hazelnut & Coffee Terrine

Hazelnut Meringue:
1 scant cup hazelnuts, coarsely
    ground
1 tablespoon all-purpose flour, sifted
1/4 cup superfine sugar
2 egg whites

Coffee Mousse:
1-1/2 (1/4-oz.) pkgs. unflavored gelatin
    (4-1/2 teaspoons)
2/3 cup double strength hot coffee
3 eggs, separated
1/4 cup superfine sugar
1-1/4 cups whipping cream

Raspberry Sauce:
8 ozs. raspberries
1/3 cup powdered sugar
1 tablespoon water
2 teaspoons lemon juice

To make hazelnut meringue, preheat oven to 350F (175C). Line a 9" x 5" x 3" loaf pan with plastic wrap. Put a piece of parchment paper the length and twice the width of pan on a baking sheet.

In a bowl, combine ground hazelnuts, flour and 1/2 of sugar. In a bowl, whisk egg whites until soft peaks form. Whisk in remaining sugar; fold in hazelnut mixture. Spread meringue mixture over parchment on baking sheet and bake in oven 20 minutes, until crisp.

To make coffee mousse, sprinkle gelatin over hot coffee; stir until dissolved. In a bowl, whisk egg yolks and superfine sugar until pale and thick. Stir in coffee.

In another bowl, whip cream until thick but not stiff. In a clean bowl, whisk egg whites until soft peaks form. Fold cream into coffee mixture, then fold in egg whites.

Cut meringue in half; place 1/2 of meringue in prepared pan. Cover with 1/2 of mousse mixture. Repeat layers. Chill overnight.

To make raspberry sauce, in a blender or food processor, puree raspberries with powdered sugar and water. Press through a sieve into a bowl; add lemon juice.

To serve, turn out meringue onto a serving dish. Cut in slices with a hot knife. Serve with raspberry sauce.

Makes 8 servings.

Walnut & Coffee Roll

Roulade:
4 eggs, separated
1/2 cup superfine sugar
1 cup finely chopped walnuts
1 tablespoon strong coffee
Superfine sugar for dusting

Filling:
2/3 cup cream cheese, softened
1 tablespoon strong coffee
2 teaspoons brandy
2 tablespoons superfine sugar
2/3 cup whipping cream

Mocha Sauce:
4 (1-oz.) squares semi-sweet chocolate,
broken in pieces
2 tablespoons unsalted butter
1/4 cup coffee

Preheat oven to 350F (175C). Line a jelly-roll pan with parchment paper.

In a bowl, whisk egg yolks and sugar until thick and light. Stir in chopped walnuts and coffee.

In a separate bowl, whisk egg whites until soft peaks form. Fold gently into walnut mixture. Spread in prepared pan and bake in oven 15 minutes, until firm. Cool in pan.

Meanwhile to make filling, in a bowl, combine cream cheese, coffee, brandy and sugar; beat until smooth. In a bowl, whip cream until it holds its shape, then fold into mixture.

Sprinkle a sheet of waxed paper with superfine sugar. Turn roulade onto paper; remove parchment paper. Spread filling over roulade, then roll up.

To make sauce, put chocolate, butter and cold coffee in a saucepan and heat gently until melted and smooth; cool.

Serve roulade cut in slices with mocha sauce poured around.

Makes 8 servings.

Walnut & Chocolate Meringue

Meringue:
4 egg whites
1-1/4 cups superfine sugar
1-1/4 cups ground walnuts

Filling:
6 (1-oz.) squares semi-sweet chocolate
3 tablespoons unsalted butter
2 tablespoons coffee
2 tablespoons brandy
3/4 cup whipping cream

To Decorate:
Chocolate leaves, see page 86

Preheat oven to 275F (140C). Line 2 baking sheets with waxed paper.

To make meringue, in a bowl, whisk egg whites until stiff. Whisk in 1/2 of sugar. In another bowl, mix remaining sugar and ground walnuts. Carefully fold into meringue mixture.

Pipe or spread meringue in 2 (8-inch) rounds on prepared baking sheets. Bake in oven about 1-1/2 hours or until completely dry. Transfer to wire racks to cool.

To make filling, melt chocolate with butter, coffee and brandy; cool. Whip cream lightly; stir in chocolate mixture.

Sandwich meringue rounds together with most of chocolate cream, reserving a little to decorate top.

Place reserved cream in a pastry bag. Pipe cream rosettes on top of meringues and decorate with chocolate leaves.

Makes 8 servings.

Variation: Make individual meringue cakes. Spread meringue in 8 (3-inch) circles and 8 (2-inch) circles. Assemble as above, using smaller circles as tops.

Tirami Su

Cake:
3 eggs
1/2 cup plus 1 tablespoon superfine
  sugar
3/4 cup all-purpose flour
1 tablespoon instant coffee granules,
  if desired

Filling:
12 ozs. mascarpone cheese
4 egg yolks
1/2 cup superfine sugar
2 tablespoons rum
2 egg whites

To Finish:
3/4 cup coffee
2 (1-oz.) squares semi-sweet chocolate,
  grated

To make cake, preheat oven to 350F (175C). Grease and line a deep 8-inch round cake pan with waxed paper.

In a bowl, whisk eggs and sugar until thick and light. Sift flour and coffee granules, if desired, over mixture, then fold in gently.

Spoon mixture into prepared pan and bake in oven 30 minutes, until golden and cake springs back when pressed in center. Turn onto a wire rack to cool.

To make filling, in a bowl, beat mascarpone until soft. In another bowl, whisk egg yolks and sugar until thick and light. Stir in mascarpone and rum. In a clean bowl, whisk egg whites until soft peaks form; fold into cheese mixture.

Cut cake horizontally in 3 layers. Put 1 layer on a serving plate. Sprinkle with 1/3 of coffee. Cover with 1/3 of filling. Repeat layers, finishing with a topping of cheese mixture. Chill overnight.

Sprinkle with grated chocolate to serve.

Makes 8 servings.

Cinnamon & Coffee Cheesecake

Crust:
6 ozs. chocolate chip cookies, finely crushed
1/4 cup unsalted butter, melted

Filling:
2 (8-oz.) pkgs. cream cheese, softened
1-1/4 cups half and half
3 eggs, beaten
1/4 cup all-purpose flour, sifted
1/3 cup superfine sugar
3 tablespoons strong coffee
1 teaspoon ground cinnamon
2 (2-oz.) squares semi-sweet chocolate, broken in pieces

Preheat oven to 350F (175C). Grease an 8-inch round springform cake pan.

To make crust, in a bowl, combine cookie crumbs and melted butter. Press mixture into bottom of prepared pan. Chill while making filling.

To make filling, in a bowl, beat cream cheese and coffee. Add eggs, flour, sugar, coffee and cinnamon; beat thoroughly. Pour onto crust.

Melt chocolate in a bowl set over a pan of hot water. Drizzle melted chocolate over top of cheesecake. Using handle of a teaspoon, swirl chocolate to give a marbled effect.

Bake in oven 50 to 60 minutes, until firm. Cool in oven with door ajar. Remove cheesecake from pan and chill 2 hours before serving.

Makes 8 servings.

Note: If desired, melted chocolate may be piped over top of cheesecake using a pastry bag fitted with a plain tip.

Brandy Alexander Pie

Pastry:
2 cups all-purpose flour
1/2 cup plus 2 tablespoons unsalted butter
3 tablespoons powdered sugar, sifted
1 egg yolk beaten with 2 tablespoons water

Filling:
1-1/2 (1/4-oz.) pkgs. unflavored gelatin (4-1/2 teaspoons)
2/3 cup double strength hot coffee
3 eggs, separated
1/4 cup superfine sugar
3 tablespoons brandy
2 tablespoons crème de cacao
2/3 cup whipping cream

Chocolate Caraque:
2 (2-oz.) squares semi-sweet chocolate, melted

To make pastry, sift flour into a bowl. Cut in butter until mixture resembles bread crumbs, then stir in powdered sugar. Stir in beaten egg yolk. Knead lightly to form a firm dough. Cover and chill 30 minutes.

Preheat oven to 400F (205C).

On a lightly floured surface, roll out pastry and line a deep 9-inch flan or pie pan. Bake blind 10 minutes. Lower temperature to 350F (175C) and bake 15 to 20 minutes, until pastry is golden; cool.

To make filling, sprinkle gelatin over hot coffee; stir until dissolved. In a bowl, whisk egg yolks and superfine sugar until pale and thick. Stir in coffee, brandy and crème de cacao. In a bowl, whip cream until thick but not stiff.

In another bowl, whisk egg whites until soft peaks form. Fold cream into coffee mixture. Gently fold in egg whites. Turn into crust and chill 2 to 3 hours.

To make chocolate caraque, pour chocolate onto a flat hard surface, spreading with a palette knife. Let stand until set. Holding blade of a knife at a 45° angle, push it along surface of chocolate to form curls. Lift caraque onto pie.

Makes 8 servings.

Praline Cheesecakes

Praline:
1/2 cup Brazil nuts
1/4 cup superfine sugar

Filling:
**1 (1/4-oz.) pkg. unflavored gelatin
  (1 tablespoon)**
**1 tablespoon instant coffee granules
  dissolved in 2 tablespoons boilng
  water**
1/2 (8-oz.) pkg. cream cheese, softened
1/4 cup superfine sugar
2 eggs, separated
1/2 cup whipping cream

Crust:
**4 ozs. shortbread cookies, finely
  crushed**
2 tablespoons unsalted butter, melted

Coffee Syrup:
1/4 cup superfine sugar
1/2 cup water
1/4 cup double strength hot coffee

To make praline, oil a baking sheet. In a heavy-bottom saucepan, gently heat Brazil nuts and sugar, stirring constantly, until sugar has dissolved. Cook, stirring constantly, until a rich golden-brown. Turn onto oiled baking sheet and let stand until completely cold and hard, then crush and set aside.

To make filling, sprinkle gelatin over hot coffee. Stir until dissolved and cool.

Oil 6 ramekins. In a bowl, beat cream cheese, sugar and egg yolks until smooth. Stir in coffee and 1/2 of praline. In another bowl, whip cream until thick; fold into cheese mixture.

In a clean bowl, whisk egg whites until soft peaks form; fold gently into cheese mixture. Spoon into oiled ramekins.

To make crust, combine cookie crumbs and melted butter. Spread over cheesecakes, pressing down gently. Chill 2 hours.

To make syrup, put sugar and water into a pan. Bring to a boil and boil rapidly 5 minutes. Stir in coffee and cool.

Turn cheesecakes out onto serving plates. Top with remaining praline and pour syrup around to serve.

Makes 6 servings.

Mille-Feuilles

4 sheets filo pastry
Powdered sugar

Crème Pâtissière:
4 eggs, separated
1/4 cup superfine sugar
1/4 cup all-purpose flour, sifted
1-1/4 cups milk
2 teaspoons instant coffee granules
1 tablespoon plus 1 teaspoon
   whipping cream

To Serve:
Strawberry fans, below

Preheat oven to 400F (205C).

Fold each sheet of pastry to make 4 layers. Cut 3 (3-inch) circles through layers to make 48 circles. Put circles on baking sheets and bake in oven 2 minutes, until golden and crisp; cool.

To make crème pâtissière, in a bowl, beat egg yolks, sugar, flour and a little of milk. In a saucepan, heat remaining milk and coffee granules until almost boilng. Pour into egg yolk mixture, stirring constantly. Return to pan and cook gently 2 to 3 minutes. Cover and cool.

In a bowl, whip cream until thick; stir into custard. In a clean bowl, whisk egg whites until soft peaks form; fold into custard.

To assemble each mille feuille, put 2 pastry rounds on top of each other on a serving dish. Carefully spread with crème pâtissière. Repeat layers twice more. Put 2 more pastry rounds on top and dust thickly with powdered sugar. Repeat until you have 6 mille feuilles, each composed of 4 double layers of pastry and 3 layers of crème pâtissière.

With a very hot skewer, mark lines on powdered sugar.

Serve immediately, decorated with strawberry fans.

Makes 6 servings.

Note: To make strawberry fans, slice strawberries almost through to stalk end, then fan out.

Mille feuilles must be served as soon as they are assembled as pastry softens very quickly.

Maple Pecan Torte

3/4 cup light-brown sugar
4 egg yolks
1-1/3 cups pecans, ground
1 tablespoon dried white bread
   crumbs
1 tablespoon strong coffee
3 egg whites

Filling:
1-1/4 cups whipping cream
1 tablespoon strong coffee
3 to 4 tablespoons maple syrup

To Decorate:
2 (1-oz.) squares semi-sweet chocolate,
   melted
8 rose leaves

Preheat oven to 350F (175C). Grease and line a deep 8-inch round cake pan with waxed paper.

In a bowl, whisk sugar and egg yolks until thick and light. Gently fold in ground nuts and bread crumbs, then stir in coffee.

In a bowl, whisk egg whites until soft peaks form; fold into mixture. Pour into prepared pan and bake in oven 25 to 30 minutes, until well risen and firm to touch. Turn onto a wire rack to cool.

To make chocolate leaves, brush chocolate over underside of rose leaves. Place on waxed paper and let stand until completely set. Peel off leaves.

To make filling, in a bowl, whip cream and coffee until thick. Stir in maple syrup.

Slice cooled cake horizontally in 2 layers and sandwich together with 1/2 of cream. Spread remaining cream over cake and decorate with chocolate leaves.

Makes 8 servings.

Mousseline Gâteau

5 eggs, separated
2/3 cup superfine sugar
1 tablespoon instant coffee granules
   dissolved in 1 tablespoon boiling
   water
1-1/4 cups ground almonds
1/3 cup ground rice

Mousseline Cream:
1/3 cup superfine sugar
3 tablespoons water
3 egg yolks
1/2 cup plus 2 tablespoons unsalted
   butter, softened
2/3 cup whipping cream

Topping:
6 (1-oz.) squares semi-sweet chocolate
2 tablespoons unsalted butter
2 tablespoons water

Preheat oven to 350F (175C). Grease and line 2 deep 8-inch round cake pans with waxed paper.

In a bowl, whisk egg yolks, sugar and coffee until thick and light. Fold in ground almonds and ground rice. In a separate bowl, whisk egg whites until soft peaks form; fold into mixture. Divide between prepared pans and bake in oven 20 to 25 minutes, until well risen and firm to touch. Turn out onto a wire rack to cool.

To make mousseline cream, put sugar and water into a saucepan and heat gently until sugar has dissolved. Bring to a boil and boil steadily until syrup reaches 230F (110C) or until a little of syrup forms a thread when pressed between a wet thumb and forefinger and drawn apart.

In a bowl, whisk egg yolks. Pour syrup onto yolks in a steady stream, whisking constantly until thick and mousse-like. Whisk in butter, a little at a time. In another bowl, whip cream until soft peaks form; fold into egg yolk mixture. Chill 1 hour.

Cut cooled cakes in half horizontally and sandwich together with mousseline cream.

To make topping, put chocolate, butter and water into a bowl set over a pan of hot water. Stir until smooth. Pour over cake, spreading over top and side. Let stand until set.

Makes 8 servings.

Halva Gâteau

Cake:
3/4 cup superfine sugar
3/4 cup unsalted butter, softened
3 eggs, beaten
1/3 cup strong coffee
1-1/2 cups plus 2 tablespoons
  semolina
1 tablespoon baking powder
1 teaspoon ground cinnamon
1-1/3 cups ground almonds

Syrup:
3/4 cup superfine sugar
1/3 cup strong coffee

Halva Cream:
4 ozs. halva, broken in pieces
3 tablespoons strong coffee
1/2 cup superfine sugar
12 tablespoons unsalted butter,
  softened

To Decorate:
1/4 cup pistachios, chopped

Preheat oven to 425F (220C). Grease
and line 2 deep 8-inch round cake
pans with waxed paper.

To make cake, in a bowl, cream
sugar and butter until light and fluffy. Gradually beat in eggs and coffee.

Stir in semolina, baking powder, cinnamon and ground almonds. Divide
between prepared pans and bake in
oven 10 minutes. Lower temperature
to 350F (175C) and bake 10 to 15
minutes, until a skewer inserted into
center comes out clean. Let stand in
pan 2 minutes, then turn each out
onto a wire rack placed over a plate.

Meanwhile, make syrup. Put sugar
and water into a saucepan and heat
gently until sugar has dissolved. Boil
4 minutes, remove from heat and stir
in coffee. Bring back to a boil, pour
over cakes and cool.

To make halva cream, in a saucepan, heat halva, coffee and sugar
gently until smooth; cool.

In a bowl, beat butter until soft,
then beat in halva mixture.

Sandwich cakes together with 1/2
of halva cream. Spread with remaining cream and decorate with nuts.

Makes 8 servings.

Note: Halva is a Greek and Turkish
confection.

Rich Cheesecake Gâteau

Cake:
3 eggs
1/2 cup plus 2 tablespoons superfine
  sugar
1/4 cup all-purpose flour
1 tablespoon instant coffee granules,
  if desired

Filling:
1/2 cup unsalted butter, softened
1 cup light-brown sugar
3 eggs, separated
1 tablespoon plus 1 teaspoon instant
  coffee granules dissolved in 2
  tablespoons water
7/8 (8-oz.) pkg. cream cheese, softened
1-1/4 cups whipping cream

To Decorate:
Sifted powdered sugar

Preheat oven to 350F (175C). Grease
and line a deep 9-inch round cake
pan with waxed paper.

To make cake, in a bowl, whisk
eggs and superfine sugar until thick
and light. Sift flour and coffee granules, if desired, over mixture, then
fold in gently.

Spoon mixture into prepared pan
and bake in oven 25 minutes, until
golden and cake springs back when
pressed in middle. Turn onto a wire
rack and cool.

Wash and dry cake pan. Line bottom and side with waxed paper.

To make filling, in a bowl, cream
butter and brown sugar until light
and fluffy. Beat in egg yolks, coffee
and cream cheese.

In a bowl, whip cream until it just
holds its shape. Fold whipped cream
into cheese mixture.

In a bowl, whisk egg whites until
stiff, fold into mixture.

Cut cake in half horizontally. Put 1
layer into prepared pan, spread filling on top, then cover with other
layer. Chill overnight.

Carefully turn cake out onto a serving plate and dust with powdered
sugar to serve.

Makes 12 to 15 servings.

Gâteau Pavé Mocha

1/2 cup unsalted butter, softened
3/4 cup powdered sugar, sifted
4 egg yolks
2 teaspoons instant coffee granules dissolved in 1 tablespoon boiling water
4 (1-oz.) squares semi-sweet chocolate, melted
1/3 cup milk
3 tablespoons medium-dry sherry
18 ladyfinger cookies

To Decorate:
Sifted powdered sugar
Chocolate caraque, see page 83

In a bowl, cream together butter and powdered sugar until light and fluffy. Beat in egg yolks, 1 at a time. Carefully stir in cooled coffee and chocolate. Mix until thoroughly blended.

In a shallow dish, mix together milk and sherry. Quickly dip in 6 ladyfingers 1 at a time, then arrange side by side on a serving dish. Cover with 1/3 of chocolate mixture. Repeat layers, then top with remaining ladyfingers. Cover top and sides of cake with remaining chocolate mixture. Chill several hours or overnight.

Sprinkle with powdered sugar and arrange chocolate caraque over top of cake. Serve cut into slices, to reveal layers.

Makes 6 servings.

Note: Refrigerate gâteau several hours after assembling to enable flavors to blend. Remove from refrigerator 1 hour before serving.

Paris Brest

Praline:
1/3 cup blanched almonds
1/4 cup superfine sugar

Choux Pastry:
1 cup all-purpose flour
1/4 cup unsalted butter
1 cup water
2 eggs plus 1 yolk, beaten
1/4 cup slivered almonds

Crème Au Beurre Filling:
3/4 cup superfine sugar
6 egg yolks
3/4 cup milk
2 tablespoons instant coffee granules
3/4 cup unsalted butter

To Finish:
Powdered sugar for sprinkling

Make praline as for Praline Coffee Ice Cream, page 56. Preheat oven to 425F (220C).

To make choux pastry, sift flour. Put butter and water into a saucepan; heat gently until butter has melted, then bring to a boil. Add flour all at once. Beat with a wooden spoon 1 minute, until mixture forms a ball and leaves side of pan clean.

Cool slightly, then add eggs, a little at a time, beating thoroughly until mixture is smooth, glossy and holds its shape. Add more or less egg, if needed.

Pipe choux mixture into 8 (3-inch) rings on dampened baking sheets. Sprinkle with almonds. Bake in oven 10 minutes. Lower temperature to 350F (175C) and bake 10 to 15 minutes, until dark golden and crisp. Cut rings in half horizontally; cool.

To make filling, in a bowl, whisk sugar and egg yolks until thick and pale. In a pan, heat milk and coffee granules until almost boiling. Slowly pour onto egg yolks, stirring thoroughly. Return to pan and cook over a low heat, stirring constantly, until thick enough to coat back of spoon. Strain into a bowl and whisk until tepid. Whisk in butter, a little at a time, whisking until thickened. Chill, then stir in praline.

To serve, sandwich choux rings together with filling and sprinkle with powdered sugar.

Makes 8 servings.

Frosted Walnut Coffee Cake

4 eggs, separated
1/2 cup superfine sugar
3/4 cup walnuts, finely chopped
1/2 cup fresh whole-wheat bread
    crumbs
1/4 cup all-purpose flour
1/2 teaspoon ground cinnamon

Coffee Filling:
1/2 cup unsalted butter, softened
1 cup powdered sugar
1 tablespoon strong coffee

American Frosting:
1-1/2 cups granulated sugar
1/3 cup water
2 egg whites
1/4 teaspoon cream of tartar

To Decorate:
Walnut halves

Preheat oven to 350F (175C). Grease and line 2 deep 8-inch round cake pans.

In a bowl, whisk together egg yolks and superfine sugar until thick and pale. Fold in walnuts, bread crumbs, sifted flour and cinnamon. Whisk egg whites until stiff; fold into mixture. Divide between prepared pans and bake in oven 30 minutes or until firm. Turn onto a wire rack to cool.

To make filling, in a bowl, cream butter, powdered sugar and coffee. Split each cake in half. Sandwich 4 cake rounds together with filling.

To make frosting, in a saucepan, combine granulated sugar and water. Stir over low heat until sugar has dissolved. Bring to a boil and boil to soft ball stage (240F/116C). To test, drop a little syrup into a cup of cold water; it should form a soft ball. Remove from heat.

In a large bowl, whisk egg whites until stiff; add cream of tartar. Pour hot syrup onto egg whites, beating constantly. Continue beating as mixture cools. Spread over top and sides of cake, pulling icing with a palette knife to raise peaks. Decorate with walnut halves. Let stand uncovered several hours or overnight for icing to set.

Makes 8 to 10 servings.

Coffee & Cinnamon Streusel Cake

Streusel Topping:
1/2 cup all-purpose flour
2 tablespoons unsalted butter
1/3 cup light-brown sugar
2 teaspoons instant coffee granules
1/4 cup finely chopped hazelnuts

Cake:
1/2 cup unsalted butter, softened
3/4 cup light-brown sugar
2 eggs, beaten
1 cup self-rising flour
1 teaspoon ground cinnamon
1 tablespoon plus 1 teaspoon milk
2 teaspoons strong coffee

To Decorate:
Sifted powdered sugar

Preheat oven to 350F (175C). Lightly grease a deep 8-inch loose-bottom fluted flan pan.

To make streusel topping, sift flour into a bowl. Cut in butter, then stir in sugar, coffee granules and chopped nuts. Set aside.

To make cake, in a bowl, cream butter and sugar until light and fluffy. Gradually beat in eggs. Sift in flour and cinnamon; fold in gently.

In a small bowl, mix milk and coffee; fold into cake mixture. Turn into prepared pan, sprinkle with streusel topping and bake in oven 30 minutes or until firm.

Dust with powdered sugar to serve.

Makes 8 servings.

Mocha Brownies

4 (1-oz.) squares semi-sweet chocolate
1/4 cup unsalted butter
1 cup dark-brown sugar
2 eggs
1 tablespoon instant coffee granules
   dissolved in 1 tablespoon hot water
3/4 cup all-purpose flour
1/2 teaspoon baking powder
Pinch of salt
1/2 cup walnuts, chopped

Preheat oven to 350F (175C). Grease and line a deep 8-inch square cake pan with waxed paper.

Melt chocolate and butter in a saucepan over low heat; cool.

In a bowl, beat sugar and eggs until thick and pale. Fold in chocolate and cooled coffee and mix thoroughly.

Sift in flour, baking powder and salt. Lightly fold into mixture, then fold in nuts.

Pour mixture into prepared pan and bake in oven 25 to 30 minutes, until firm.

Cool in pan 30 minutes. Cut in 16 squares to serve.

Makes 16 brownies.

Note: The brownies will sink slightly when removed from pan. They should be moist in center.

Variations: Replace walnuts with chopped pecans or Brazil nuts.

Omit coffee and flavor mixture with 1/2 teaspoon ground cinnamon, added with flour.

Meringue-Topped Cake

Cake:
2/3 cup milk
2 tablespoons instant coffee granules
1/2 cup unsalted butter, softened
3/4 cup light-brown sugar
1 egg plus 2 yolks, beaten
1-1/2 cups self-rising flour, sifted
1 teaspoon ground cinnamon

Topping:
2 egg whites
1/2 cup plus 1 teaspoon superfine sugar
1/2 teaspoon ground cinnamon
1 tablespoon shredded coconut

Preheat oven to 325F (260C). Grease and line a deep 8-inch loose-bottomed square cake pan.

Heat milk in a pan until warm. Stir in coffee granules until dissolved; cool.

In a bowl, cream butter and brown sugar until light and fluffy. Gradually beat in egg. Fold in flour and cinnamon alternately with coffee-flavored milk. Turn mixture into prepared pan.

To make topping, in a bowl, whisk egg whites until soft peaks form. Gradually whisk in 1/2 cup of superfine sugar. Spread over cake mixture.

In a bowl, mix remaining 1 teaspoon of sugar, cinnamon and coconut; sprinkle over meringue. Bake in oven 50 to 55 minutes or until a fine skewer inserted into the center comes out clean and meringue is crisp.

Cool in pan 5 minutes, then carefully remove and cool on a wire rack. Serve warm or cold on day of making, cut in 9 squares.

Makes 9 servings.
Note: If you do not have a loose-bottomed pan, line a deep 8-inch square cake pan with waxed paper and allow paper to extend above sides of pan. Use paper to help lift cake out of pan.

Coffee Almond Ring

Praline:
1/3 cup blanched almonds
1/4 cup superfine sugar

Cake:
1-1/2 cups self-rising flour
1 teaspoon baking powder
1 cup light-brown sugar
3/4 cup margarine, softened
3 eggs, beaten
1/4 cup ground almonds

Syrup:
1/2 cup granulated sugar
2/3 cup water
2 teaspoons instant coffee granules
2 tablespoons brandy

To Decorate:
1 cup whipping cream

Make praline as for Praline Coffee Ice Cream, see page 56.

Preheat oven to 375F˙ (190C). Grease and flour a 9-inch tube pan.

To make cake, sift flour and baking powder into a bowl. Add brown sugar, margarine, eggs and ground almonds and beat thoroughly. Turn into prepared pan and bake in oven 25 to 30 minutes or until well risen and just firm to touch.

To make syrup, in a saucepan, put granulated sugar and water. Stir over low heat until sugar has dissolved. Bring to a boil, lower heat and simmer 3 minutes. Add coffee and brandy; stir until coffee is dissolved. Prick surface of hot cake with a skewer; pour over 1/2 of syrup. Let soak 30 minutes. Turn cake onto a plate; spoon over remaining syrup and cool.

Whip cream and spread 1/2 of whipping cream over top and side of cake. Pipe remaining cream on top and decorate with crushed praline.

Makes 6 to 8 servings.

Caramel Coffee Cake

Cake:
4 eggs
1/2 cup superfine sugar
1 cup self-rising flour, sifted
2 tablespoons instant coffee granules
   dissolved in 1 tablespoon hot water
3 tablespoons sunflower oil

Caramel Topping:
3/4 cup superfine sugar
1/4 cup plus 1 tablespoon water
1 cup powdered sugar, sifted
1/4 cup plus 2 tablespoons unsalted
   butter, softened

Preheat oven to 350F (175C). Grease and line 2 deep 8-inch round cake pans with waxed paper.

In a bowl, whisk eggs and superfine sugar until light and thick. Gently fold in flour, coffee and oil. Divide mixture between prepared pans and bake in oven 20 minutes or until well risen and golden-brown. Turn onto a wire rack to cool.

To make caramel topping, heat superfine sugar and 1/4 cup of water in a saucepan until sugar has dissolved. Bring to a boil, then cook until syrup turns a dark golden-brown. Pour all but 2 tablespoons over 1 cake. Mark in 8 sections with an oiled knife before caramel sets.

Stir 1 tablespoon of water into remaining caramel, returning to heat, if necessary, to soften caramel; cool.

In a bowl, cream powdered sugar, butter and cooled caramel. Spread over remaining cake and place caramel-topped cake on top.

Makes 8 servings.

Poppyseed Kugelhupf

2 cups all-purpose flour, sifted
1/4 cup superfine sugar
1 (1/4-oz.) pkg. fast-rising yeast
2 tablespoons poppy seeds
3 tablespoons tepid strong coffee
1/2 cup unsalted butter, melted
3 eggs, beaten

Cinnamon Butter:
1/2 cup unsalted butter, softened
Grated peel of 1/2 orange
1 teaspoon ground cinnamon

To Finish:
Powdered sugar

Grease an 8-inch kugelhupf mold.

In a bowl, mix flour, superfine sugar, yeast and poppy seeds. Heat coffee and butter to 125F to 130F (50C to 55C) and stir into dry ingredients. Stir in eggs and beat well until thoroughly blended and smooth. Cover bowl with plastic wrap and let stand in a warm place 2 to 3 hours, until doubled in size.

Stir mixture and turn into prepared mold. Cover with plastic wrap and let stand again 2 to 3 hours, until doubled in size. Preheat oven to 400F (205C).

Remove plastic wrap. Bake bread in oven 20 minutes. Lower oven temperature to 375F (190C) and bake 10 minutes more, until well risen and golden-brown. Let stand in pan 10 minutes, then turn out and cool on a wire rack.

Meanwhile, to make cinnamon butter, in a bowl, beat butter, orange peel and cinnamon until light and fluffy. Chill until required.

Dust kugelhupf with powdered sugar. Serve still slightly warm, sliced and spread with cinnamon butter.

Makes 12 to 16 servings.

Note: A kugelhupf mold is round and has a ray-like pattern on bottom and side.

Glossy Fruit Loaf

1/3 cup raisins
3/4 cup coarsely chopped dried
    peaches
1/3 cup chopped dates
1/3 cup cold Assam tea
1/2 cup unsalted butter, softened
3/4 cup light-brown sugar
2 eggs, beaten
1-1/2 cups self-rising flour, sifted
1/3 cup glacé pineapple, coarsely
    chopped
1/2 cup glacé cherries, halved
3/4 cup coarsely chopped Brazil nuts

Topping:
1/3 cup walnut halves
1/4 cup Brazil nuts
1/3 cup glacé cherries, halved
2 tablespoons apricot jam, sieved

Put raisins, peaches and dates in a bowl. Pour over tea, cover and soak overnight.

Preheat oven to 325F (160C). Grease and line a 9" x 5" x 3" loaf pan.

In a bowl, cream butter and sugar until light and fluffy. Gradually add eggs, then fold in flour alternately with soaked fruit. Gently stir in pineapple, cherries and chopped nuts.

Turn into prepared pan and arrange walnuts, Brazil nuts and cherries on top. Bake in oven 1-1/2 to 1-3/4 hours, until a skewer inserted into center of cake comes out clean.

Transfer to a wire rack to cool. Warm apricot jam and brush over top of cake.

Makes 10 servings.

Coffee & Caraway Rolls

3 cups bread flour
1 teaspoon salt
2/3 (1/4-oz.) pkg. fast-rising yeast
   (2 teaspoons)
2 teaspoons caraway seeds
1/4 cup butter
3/4 cup milk
2 tablespoons instant coffee granules
1 teaspoon superfine sugar

To Glaze:
1 egg, beaten
1 teaspoon caraway seeds

Grease a baking sheet.

Sift flour and salt into a bowl. Stir in yeast and caraway seeds.

In a small saucepan, gently heat butter, milk and coffee to 125F to 130F (50C to 55C). Add sugar and stir until dissolved.

Make a well in center of flour, pour in liquid ingredients and mix thoroughly. Knead well on a lightly floured surface until dough is smooth and elastic. Put in a large bowl, cover loosely with plastic wrap and let stand in a warm place about 2 hours, until doubled in size.

Knead lightly on floured surface 2 to 3 minutes. Divide dough in 8 pieces. Roll each piece in a thin "sausage" and tie in a knot in center. Place on prepared baking sheet. Cover and let stand in a warm place 45 minutes or until doubled in size.

Preheat oven to 400F (205C).

Brush rolls with beaten egg and sprinkle with caraway seeds. Bake in oven 15 to 20 minutes, until golden and firm.

Makes 8 rolls.

Note: These rolls are not sweet; they may be served either with savory or sweet food.

To make a loaf, put mixture in a 7-1/2" x 3-3/4" x 2-1/4" loaf pan and bake about 30 minutes, until golden and firm.

Ginger & Coffee Buns

Topping:
2 tablespoons butter
1/3 cup light-brown sugar
1 tablespoon syrup from stem ginger
2 tablespoons stem ginger, finely
chopped

Buns:
2-1/2 cups bread flour
1/2 (1/4-oz.) pkg. fast-rising yeast
(1-1/2 teaspoons)
1/4 cup butter
3/4 cup milk
1 tablespoon plus 1 teaspoon instant
coffee granules
1/3 cup light-brown sugar

Lightly grease a deep 8-inch round cake pan.

To make topping, put butter, sugar and ginger syrup in a small saucepan. Heat gently until butter has melted and sugar is dissolved. Stir in ginger. Pour into prepared pan; set aside.

To make buns, sift flour into a large bowl. Stir in yeast and cut in 1/2 of butter. In a small saucepan, heat milk to 125F to 130F (50C to 55C). Add 2 teaspoons of coffee granules and stir

ture and mix to a smooth dough. Knead on a lightly floured surface until smooth and elastic. Place in a large bowl, cover with plastic wrap and let stand in a warm place about 2 hours, until doubled in size.

Knead again 2 to 3 minutes. Roll out to a 13" x 10" rectangle. Melt remaining butter; brush over dough. Sprinkle with sugar and remaining coffee granules.

Starting from a short side, roll up dough like a jelly roll. Cut in 8 equal pieces. Place 1 piece in center of pan on topping mixture; arrange remaining slices around it. Cover with plastic wrap and let stand in a warm place about 45 minutes, until well risen. Preheat oven to 400F (205C).

Bake in oven about 25 minutes or until golden. Cool in pan 5 minutes; then turn out onto a serving plate. Pull buns apart and serve warm or cold on day they are made.

Makes 8 buns.

Coffee Almond Shortcake

Shortbread:
2 cups all-purpose flour
2 tablespoons unsalted butter
1/2 cup superfine sugar

Marzipan Filling:
2/3 cup ground almonds
1/3 cup superfine sugar
1/2 cup powdered sugar
1 egg yolk
2 teaspoons strong coffee

To Decorate:
About 2 tablespoons blanched
almonds

Preheat oven to 325F (160C). Butter a 9-inch loose-bottom flan or pie pan.

To make shortbread, sift flour into a bowl. Cut in butter, then stir in superfine sugar. Knead to form a firm dough.

To make marzipan, in a bowl, mix ground almonds, superfine sugar and powdered sugar. Stir in egg yolk and coffee, adding a little more cof-

fee, if necessary, to make a firm mixture. On a lightly floured surface, roll out marzipan to form a circle slightly smaller than diameter of prepared pan.

Divide shortbread in 2 portions, 1 slightly larger than other. Roll out larger piece and press over bottom and side of pan. Lay marzipan on top. Roll out second piece of dough to fit pan and place on top of marzipan; press firmly together around edge.

Press almonds on top of shortcake. Bake in oven 45 to 50 minutes or until golden-brown and firm. Cool in pan. Remove from pan and cut in wedges to serve.

Makes 6 to 8 servings.

Variation: Vary the decoration according to the occasion. At Christmas a pattern of glacé cherries, angelica and almonds is attractive.

Almond Coffee Slices

1-1/2 cups all-purpose flour
1/4 cup superfine sugar
1 tablespoon instant coffee granules
1/2 cup unsalted butter
1/4 cup ground almonds
Beaten egg to glaze
1/4 cup sliced almonds
1 tablespoon granulated sugar

Preheat oven to 350F (175C). Grease a jelly-roll pan.

Sift flour into a bowl. Stir in superfine sugar and coffee granules. Cut in butter until mixture forms a light dough; work in ground almonds towards end.

Press dough into prepared pan. Brush surface with beaten egg and sprinkle evenly with sliced almonds and granulated sugar. Bake in oven 20 minutes or until golden-brown.

Cool in pan 10 minutes. Cut in 18 fingers and transfer to a wire rack to cool completely.

Makes 18 slices.

Note: This is delicious served with ice cream and strawberries.

Variation: Omit sliced almonds and sugar topping. Melt 2 (1-oz.) squares semi-sweet chocolate and cool. Drizzle over top when cool and let set before removing slices from pan.

Cannoli

Pastry:
1-1/2 cups all-purpose flour
2 tablespoons powdered sugar
2 tablespoons unsalted butter
2 tablespoons sweet sherry
2 tablespoons strong coffee
Vegetable oil for deep-frying

Filling:
10 ozs. mascarpone cheese
1/3 cup powdered sugar, sifted
1/4 cup chopped pistachios
1/3 cup chopped glacé fruits

To Decorate:
Sifted powdered sugar

To make pastry, sift flour and powdered sugar into a bowl. Cut in butter, then stir in sherry and coffee. Mix to a firm dough, knead lightly, cover and chill 30 minutes.

On a lightly floured surface, roll out pastry as thinly as possible. Cut out 14 (3-1/2-inch) squares. Lightly grease several cream-horn molds. Wrap a square of pastry around each mold, forming a cone. Moisten edges with water to seal.

Deep-fry 3 or 4 cannoli at a time on molds 1 to 2 minutes, until crisp and golden. Drain on paper towels. Remove from molds and let stand until completely cold.

To make filling, in a bowl, beat mascarpone, powdered sugar, nuts and glacé fruits. Use to fill cannoli. Dust with powdered sugar. Serve within 1 to 2 hours of filling.

Makes 14 cannoli.

Note: Cannoli are traditionally made on tube-shaped molds which are available in some kitchen stores. Lengths of 1-inch dowelling could be used as an alternative.

Turkish Shortbread Bracelets

2/3 cup walnut halves
1/2 cup unsalted butter, softened
2 tablespoons superfine sugar
1 small egg yolk
1-1/2 teaspoons instant coffee
   granules dissolved in 1 teaspoon
   hot water
1-1/2 teaspoons brandy
1/4 cup cornstarch, sifted
1-1/4 cups all-purpose flour, sifted

To Decorate:
1 to 2 tablespoons strong coffee
3/4 cup powdered sugar, sifted

Preheat oven to 325F (160C). In a food processor, grind walnuts coarsely.

In a bowl, beat butter and powdered sugar until light and fluffy. Gradually add egg yolk, coffee and brandy. Stir in ground walnuts, cornstarch and flour to make a firm, soft dough; knead lightly.

On a lightly floured surface, divide dough in 16 pieces and roll each piece in a ball, then in a 7-inch rope. Form rope in a circle, pressing ends together firmly. Place slightly apart on baking sheets and bake in oven 20 minutes, until firm. Transfer to a wire rack to cool.

Brush each cookie lightly with coffee, then sprinkle with powdered sugar until thickly coated. Store loosely packed in a container with remaining powdered sugar.

Makes 16 cookies.

Variation: This type of cookie is traditionally made in a crescent shape.

Almonds or hazelnuts could be used instead of walnuts.

Pretzels

1/2 cup unsalted butter, softened
1/2 cup powdered sugar
1 egg, beaten
2 cups all-purpose flour, sifted
1 tablespoon instant coffee granules

To Decorate:
1 egg white
1 tablespoon sugar crystals

In a bowl, cream butter and powdered sugar, until thick and light. Gradually beat in egg, then stir in flour and coffee granules. Form dough in a ball, wrap in plastic wrap and chill 1 hour.

Preheat oven to 375F (190C). Grease several baking sheets.

On a lightly floured surface, divide mixture in 32 pieces. Roll in balls, then roll each ball in an 11-inch-long rope. Bend each rope in a loop. Fold ends inwards, pressing them together and onto inside of ring, to make a pretzel shape.

Brush pretzels with egg white and sprinkle with sugar crystals. Place on prepared baking sheets. Chill each batch of pretzels, while shaping remainder. Bake in oven 12 to 15 minutes, until crisp and golden. Transfer to a wire rack to cool. Store in an airtight container when cold.

Makes 32 pretzels.

Palmiers

8 ozs. puff pastry
Superfine sugar for dredging
1/4 cup superfine sugar
1 tablespoon instant coffee granules

Preheat oven to 375F (190C).

Roll out pastry to a 12" x 8" rectangle on a surface dredged with superfine sugar.

In a bowl, mix 1/4 cup superfine sugar and coffee granules. Sprinkle 1/2 of mixture over pastry. Fold long edges of pastry into middle, then fold long sides together.

On sugared surface, roll pastry out again to same size. Sprinkle with remaining sugar and coffee mixture. Fold long edges into middle; fold into middle again, then press together with a rolling pin.

Cut dough in 1/2-inch pieces. Place on baking sheets, allowing room to spread and flatten slightly. Bake in oven 15 to 20 minutes, turning over halfway through baking, until crisp and golden. Remove from baking sheets immediately and cool on wire racks.

Makes 30 pieces.

Variation: To make pinwheel cookies, roll up pastry after it has been rolled out to a rectangle the second time and cut in thin rounds.

Crispy Hazelnut Bites

Praline:
1/2 cup hazelnuts
3/4 cup superfine sugar

2 egg whites
1-1/3 cups ground hazelnuts
1 tablespoon instant coffee granules
3 tablespoons cornstarch, sifted
2 tablespoons powdered sugar, sifted

To make praline, oil a baking sheet. In a small saucepan, heat whole hazelnuts and superfine sugar gently until sugar has dissolved, then bring to a boil and cook steadily to a golden caramel. Turn onto prepared baking sheet and cool. Crush to a powder in a food processor; set aside.

Preheat oven to 375F (190C). Line 2 baking sheets with parchment paper.

In a bowl, whisk egg whites until foamy. In another bowl, mix crushed praline, ground hazelnuts, coffee granules and cornstarch. Stir in enough egg white to give a firm dough. Knead lightly.

Roll pieces of dough in balls, each the size of a small walnut. Roll in remaining egg white then in powdered sugar. Place on prepared baking sheets and bake in oven 15 minutes, until puffed up and golden. Cool slightly, then transfer to wire racks to cool completely.

Store in a single layer in airtight containers.

Makes 20 pieces.

Coffee Macaroons

2 egg whites
1/2 cup superfine sugar
1-1/4 cups ground almonds, sifted
1 tablespoon ground rice or
   cornstarch
1 tablespoon instant coffee granules

To Decorate:
3 (1-oz.) squares semi-sweet chocolate,
   broken in pieces

Preheat oven to 300F (150C). Line several baking sheets with parchment paper.

In a bowl, whisk egg whites until soft peaks form.

In a second bowl, mix sugar, ground almonds, ground rice and coffee granules. Carefully fold into egg whites, then mix well, until smooth.

Roll in 18 balls, each the size of a small walnut. Place on prepared bak-ing sheets and press lightly to flatten. Bake in oven 25 to 30 minutes, until golden. Cool on baking sheets. When cold tear away surplus rice paper from each macaroon.

To decorate, melt chocolate in a bowl set over a pan of hot water; stir until smooth. Spread chocolate over 1/2 of top of each macaroon. Let stand until set.

Makes 18 macaroons.

Variations: Ground hazelnuts may be used instead of ground almonds.

Instead of decorating macaroons with melted chocolate, press a split almond or halved glacé cherry onto each macaroon before baking.

Tiny macaroons can be made to serve as petit fours.

Viennese Cookies

1 cup plus 2 tablespoons all-purpose
 flour
2 tablespoons cocoa powder
1/2 cup unsalted butter, softened
1/3 cup powdered sugar, sifted

Coating:
3-1/2 (1-oz.) squares semi-sweet
 chocolate, melted

Coffee Butter Icing:
1/4 cup unsalted butter, softened
1 cup powdered sugar, sifted
2 teaspoons strong coffee
2 teaspoons milk

To Finish:
Powdered sugar

Preheat oven to 350F (175C). Grease
2 baking sheets.

Sift flour and cocoa together. In a
bowl, cream butter and powdered
sugar until light and fluffy. Add flour
and cocoa and work until mixture is
smooth and a piping consistency.
Spoon into a pastry bag fitted with a
1-inch fluted nozzle.

Pipe 2-1/2-inch lengths of mixture
onto prepared baking sheets, allowing space for cookies to spread. Bake
in oven 15 minutes or until firm. Cool
on baking sheets a few minutes, then
transfer cookies to a wire rack to cool
completely.

Dip ends of each cookie into melted
chocolate and let stand in a cool place
to set.

To make coffee butter icing, in a
bowl, beat butter with 1/2 of powdered sugar until smooth. Add
remaining powdered sugar, coffee
and milk; beat thoroughly. Sandwich
cookies together in pairs with icing.
Sprinkle with powdered sugar to
serve.

Makes about 15 cookies.

Variations: Sprinkle chopped nuts
onto chocolate-coated ends of cookies
while chocolate is still soft.

Pipe cookie mixture in rosette
shapes, top with melted chocolate
and decorate each with a hazelnut or
walnut.

Coffee Cream Cookies

Cookies:
1/4 cup butter, softened
1/4 cup superfine sugar
1 egg, beaten
2 teaspoons instant coffee granules
1-1/2 cups all-purpose flour
1/2 cup cornstarch
1/2 teaspoon baking powder

To Decorate:
2 (1-oz.) squares semi-sweet chocolate, melted

Coffee Filling:
1/4 cup unsalted butter, softened
3/4 cup powdered sugar, sifted
1 egg yolk
1 teaspoon instant coffee granules

Preheat oven to 350F (175C). Grease 3 or 4 baking sheets.

In a bowl, beat butter and sugar until light and fluffy. In another bowl, beat egg with coffee granules until dissolved, then add to creamed mixture gradually, beating well. Sift flour, cornstarch and baking powder over mixture. Stir in to make a soft dough; knead lightly.

On a floured surface, roll out dough to a 1/8-inch thickness. Using a 2-inch fluted cutter, cut out cookies and place on prepared baking sheets. Bake in oven 10 to 15 minutes, until firm and lightly browned. Transfer to wire racks to cool.

Put cooled melted chocolate into a pastry bag, snip off end and pipe parallel zigzag lines on 1/2 of cookies.

To make filling, in a bowl, beat butter and powdered sugar until smooth and creamy. In another bowl, mix egg yolk with coffee granules; add to creamed mixture and beat until smooth.

Spread filling on plain cookies and sandwich together with decorated cookies. Let stand in a cool place until filling is firm.

Makes about 24 cookies.

Note: These cookies are best eaten within 2 days of filling.

Variation: Omit chocolate decoration; dust cookies with sifted powdered sugar.

Coffee Creams

2 cups granulated sugar
2/3 cup water
Pinch of cream of tartar
3 tablespoons half and half
1/2 teaspoon strong coffee

To Finish:
3 (1-oz.) squares semi-sweet chocolate

Combine sugar and water in a heavy-bottom saucepan. Heat gently until sugar has dissolved. Bring to a boil. Add cream of tartar. Boil syrup to 240F (116C) or until a few drops of syrup form a soft ball when dropped into a cup of cold water. Stir in half and half.

Sprinkle a little water on a work surface or marble board. Pour syrup onto surface or board and let stand a few minutes to cool.

When a skin forms around edges, collect syrup with a spatula. Turn mixture, working it backwards and forwards in a figure-8 movement, until it becomes opaque and grainy, then knead in coffee.

Pull off pieces of fondant the size of small walnut. Roll in a ball, then press to flatten slightly. Let stand overnight to dry.

To finish, melt chocolate in a bowl set over a pan of hot water. Dip 1 end of each coffee cream into chocolate to half-coat. Place on waxed paper to dry.

Makes 20 pieces.

Variation: Instead of coating coffee creams with chocolate, press half a walnut or pecan on top or drizzle with melted chocolate.

Brandy Coffee Cups

Chocolate Cups:
5 (1-oz.) squares semi-sweet chocolate, broken in pieces
1 teaspoon sunflower oil

Filling:
2/3 cup whipping cream
1 tablespoon instant coffee granules
6 (1-oz.) squares white chocolate, broken in small pieces
2 teaspoons brandy

To make chocolate cups, put chocolate and oil in a bowl set over a pan of hot water. Let stand until melted, then stir until smooth.

Spread melted chocolate evenly over inside of 20 double thickness of petit four cups. Chill until set. Remelt chocolate, if necessary. Spread a second layer of chocolate in cups. Chill until completely set. Carefully remove paper cups.

To make filling, in a saucepan, heat whipping cream and coffee granules to boiling point, stirring until coffee has dissolved; remove from heat. Add white chocolate and stir until smooth. Return to low heat and stir until mixture begins to bubble. Gradually stir in brandy; cool.

Beat chocolate cream until thick. Spoon into a pastry bag fitted with a large star nozzle and pipe into chocolate cups.

Store in refrigerator. Use within 2 to 3 days.

Makes 20 pieces.

Variations: White chocolate could be used for chocolate cups.

Semi-sweet chocolate may be used in filling.

Brandy may be substituted with Tia Maria or Kahlùa or omitted altogether.

Pistachio & Coffee Fudge

1-1/4 cups milk
4 cups granulated sugar
1 cup unsalted butter
2 tablespoons instant coffee granules
2 tablespoons light corn syrup
1 (14-oz.) can sweetened condensed
  milk
1/2 cup chopped pistachios

Grease a jelly-roll pan.

In a large saucepan, put milk, sugar and butter. Stir over gentle heat until sugar has dissolved. Stir in coffee granules, syrup and condensed milk; bring to a boil. Boil steadily until mixture reaches soft ball stage (240F/116C). To test, drop a spoonful of mixture into cold water—a soft ball should form. Cool 5 minutes.

Beat vigorously with a wooden spoon until mixture begins to thicken. Stir in pistachio nuts. Continue beating until mixture has a fudge-like texture. Quickly pour into prepared pan and let stand in a cool place to set. Cut fudge in squares to serve.

Makes about 3 pounds.

Variations: Chopped walnuts, Brazil nuts, almonds, pecan nuts or hazelnuts may be used instead of pistachios.

Chocolate Fudge: Substitute 2 tablespoons cocoa powder for instant coffee granules.

Mocha Fudge: Add 1 tablespoon cocoa powder with coffee.

Mocha Tia Maria Truffles

8 (1-oz.) squares semi-sweet chocolate,
 broken in pieces
2 egg yolks
2 tablespoons unsalted butter
2 teaspoons Tia Maria
2 tablespoons whipping cream
2 teaspoons instant coffee granules

Coating:
3 (1-oz.) squares semi-sweet or white
 chocolate, melted

Melt 8 squares chocolate in a bowl set over a pan of hot water; stir until smooth.

Add egg yolks, butter, Tia Maria, whipping cream and coffee granules and stir until mixture is thick. Remove bowl from pan, cool, then chill until firm enough to handle.

Scoop out teaspoonfuls of chocolate mixture and roll in balls. Dip in melted chocolate to coat and use a palette knife to create a rough surface. Let stand on a wire rack until set.

Store in refrigerator. Use within 2 to 3 days.

Makes 14 to 16 pieces.

Variations: Brandy, rum or Kahlùa may be used instead of Tia Maria.

Truffles could be made with white instead of semi-sweet chocolate.

Truffles may be coated in grated semi-sweet or white chocolate. Alternatively, truffles may be rolled in cocoa powder, instant coffee granules or a mixture of sifted powdered sugar and coffee granules.

Tea Refreshers

Strawberry Cup
1 oz. Darjeeling tea
2-1/2 cups lukewarm water
1-1/4 cups sparkling white wine, well
    chilled
3/4 cup ginger ale
Ice cubes
8 ozs. strawberries, sliced

Put tea into a pitcher or bowl, pour over warm water and let stand overnight to infuse.

Strain into a large pitcher. Add wine and ginger ale and stir well. Put ice cubes and strawberries into 8 glasses. Pour over tea mixture.

Makes 8 servings.

Planters Punch
1 oz. Darjeeling tea
2-1/2 cups lukewarm water
2-1/2 cups sparkling apple juice
Juice of 2 limes
2/3 cup brandy
Ice cubes

To Decorate:
Apple and lime slices

Put tea into a pitcher or bowl, pour over warm water and let stand overnight to infuse.

Strain into a large pitcher. Add apple juice, lime juice and brandy and stir thoroughly. Chill well. Pour into glasses, add ice cubes and decorate with fruit to serve.

Makes 12 servings.

Iced Tea
1-1/2 ozs. Darjeeling tea
4 cups lukewarm water
Sprig of mint
1 lemon, sliced
Ice cubes
Superfine sugar, if desired

Put tea into a pitcher or bowl, pour over warm water and let stand overnight to infuse.

Strain tea into a large pitcher and add remaining ingredients. Pour into glasses to serve.

Makes 6 servings.

Tea Revivers

Irish Mist
**1-1/4 cups freshly made Irish
  Breakfast tea**
1/3 cup Irish whiskey
Honey to taste
1/4 cup whipping cream
Grated nutmeg for sprinkling

Heat tea and whiskey in a saucepan
until hot but not boiling. Stir in honey. Pour into small cups. Slowly and
carefully pour 1 tablespoon of whipping cream over back of a teaspoon
into each cup, so that it floats on top.
Sprinkle with grated nutmeg.

Makes 4 servings.

Winter Warmer
1 tablespoon rum
1 cup freshly made Ceylon tea
1 slice orange
1 cinnamon stick
2 cloves

Stir rum into tea. Add orange slice,
cinnamon stick and cloves and serve.

Makes 1 serving.

Spicy Punch
2-1/2 cups hot China tea
2-1/2 cups red wine
1/4 cup sugar
1 cinnamon stick
6 cloves
1/2 lemon, sliced
1/3 cup brandy

Heat tea and wine in a saucepan to
just below boiling point. Add sugar,
cinnamon stick, cloves and lemon.
Cover pan and let stand 5 minutes to
infuse. Stir in brandy. Serve in heat-
proof glasses.

Makes 10 servings.

Coffee Cocktails

Café Brûlot
4 cloves
Strip of lemon peel
Strip of orange peel
1/2 cinnamon stick
1 tablespoon light-brown sugar
1/4 cup brandy
2 cups hot freshly made coffee

In a bowl, put cloves, lemon and orange peel, cinnamon and sugar. In a ladle, warm brandy; light and pour into bowl. Stir until sugar has dissolved. Slowly pour in hot coffee, stirring constantly. Ladle into warmed cups and serve.

Makes 4 servings.

Café de Olla
4 cups water
1/2 cup dark-brown sugar
1 (2-inch) cinnamon stick
4 cloves
2/3 cup dark roasted ground coffee

In a saucepan, heat water, sugar, cinnamon and cloves, stirring occasionally, until sugar has dissolved; bring to a boil. Remove from heat and stir in coffee. Allow to settle, then bring to a boil. Remove from heat. Cover pan and let stand in warm place for grounds to settle. Strain into earthenware mugs.

Makes 6 servings.

Almond Coffee
1 teaspoon light-brown sugar
2 tablespoons amaretto liqueur
1/2 cup hot freshly made coffee
Whipped cream
1 teaspoon slivered almonds, toasted

Put sugar into a heatproof glass; add Amaretto. Pour in coffee. To serve, top with whipped cream; sprinkle with almonds.

Makes 1 serving.

Coffee Cocktails

Café Alexander
Crushed ice
2 tablespoons strong coffee, chilled
and sweetened to taste
2 tablespoons crème de cacao
2 tablespoons plus 2 teaspoons
brandy
2 tablespoons whipping cream,
chilled
Chocolate curls

Put crushed ice into a cocktail shaker.
Add coffee, crème de cacao, brandy
and cream. Shake well; strain into a
glass. Top with chocolate curls to
serve.

Makes 1 serving.

Gaelic Coffee
1 teaspoon light-brown sugar
2 tablespoons Irish whiskey
1/2 cup hot freshly made coffee
2 tablespoons whipping cream

Put sugar into a heatproof glass; add
whiskey. Pour in coffee. Dip a teaspoon into coffee to warm it, then
carefully pour cream over back of
spoon to float on coffee.

Makes 1 serving.

Jamaican Coffee
Ice cubes
3/4 cup strong coffee, chilled
1/4 cup dark rum
2 tablespoons whipping cream
Grated nutmeg

Put several ice cubes into a tall glass.
In a bowl, combine chilled coffee and
rum. Pour over ice cubes. Top with
whipped cream and sprinkle with
grated nutmeg. Serve immediately
with straws.

Makes 1 serving.

Index